DARK PSYCHOLOGY SECRETS

Learn how to manipulate and influence people, develop secret techniques for emotional and mind control and learn how to brainwash and how to defend yourself.

AUTOR:

BRANDON FILIP, PETER COOPER

BOOK DESCRIPTION

Dark Psychology is a powerful tool that has always been used by the most influential people of the world both historically and presently. A lot of people are unaware of the impact of this tool on them; indeed, many do not know that they are victims of Dark Psychology. Even you, the reader, have once fallen to the power of the Dark Psychology; but do not falter, it is consolable to know that almost everyone in the world has become victims of this art either directly or indirectly. Powerful psychologists and psychological manipulators alike had once become victims of the deception, but they learned to grow out of it and used the tool to their own advantage. Now you should consider yourself fortunate that, by reading what is contained in this book, you will never be a victim of manipulation anymore; instead, you will become a master of the art of Dark Psychology. But how you choose to apply it on people around you is entirely up to you.

This book contains some extreme principles of dark psychology which are not for people who have a high moral standard to themselves. You should be warned that the details contained in this book may challenge your perception of what you consider right or wrong. It is not at all for the faint of heart; and if you are not strong enough, after reading a few of its chapters, you may be forced to close it in disgust and consider it a demonic element. But there is nothing demonic about it, every subject touched in this book is real and there have been various genuine cases of the manipulative effects of the application of the Dark Psychology.

Topics like Mind Control, Hypnotism, Seduction, Dark Persuasion Technics, Covert Manipulation Methods, Deceptive Tactics, The Dark Triad, Brainwashing, and various other topics are discussed in details in this book. Every chapter is explained in such a simple way that the layman can easily understand, especially one without zero scientific knowledge.

Various concepts detailed in this book are backed up with relevant illustrations to make understanding of the chapter a lot better. There are also various historical references that support the claims of some principles that may seem far-fetched, especially to some radically innocent minds.

The case studies contained in this book have been introduced to make the reader understand further how the minds of some criminally insane people work, including what motivated them to carry out the gruesome crimes they committed. However, it is not everything in this book that focuses on the evil of the human mind. Like it has already been established in the introductory chapters, the principles of Dark Psychology can be applied for either evil or a good purpose, and whatever the reader intends to use it for lies solely on his own choice.

Most importantly, you should understand that, after reading this book, you will never fall victim to the principles of Sark Psychology *again*, for you will already have been familiar with all the techniques there are.

CONTENTS

INTRODUCTION

Everything that happens in the world – business, relationships, science, manipulation, deception – begins from the mind; it usually occurs in the mind frame, which can rightly be referred to as the power station of the entire body.

The "mind frame", however, is a mental level that defines certain outcomes and the environments where something happens. The mind frame gives the premises of a happening – either a positive occurrence or the negative. Therefore, the mind can be regarded as the power-station of a person's choice, or his influence on another. Some minds are stronger than others, obviously. That is why we see some people dominating the lives of other people. Usually, the power of the mind, not the strength, makes a person who he is. In this case, the strongest frame of mind is the one that defines the outcome between two or more people. Sometimes, you find yourself interacting with another person and you have no choice than to suck that individual into your own frame, usually in a way to make them submissive to you, and this is where the theory of manipulation sets in. Most times, an individual tries to exercise his own mind frame on another individual in such a way that the second party is manipulated into a level of submission. This usually occurs between people of opposing sexes. A husband would want to exercise his masculinity on his own wife and demands that the wife submits. This submission can be achieved either by mere brute force or by the intelligent application of the psychology of manipulation – which, of course, is usually more effective than the former. How was Hitler able to marshal all of Germany beyond into following him? How? Surely, he did not strap san atomic bomb on himself and demand that they follow him or he would blow everyone to smithereens. If he had done that, he would have either been disarmed and then thrown into a jail where he would never see the light of day again until he died, or someone in the crowd would have simply shot him on the forehead because he would be regarded as a madman. Adolf knew all these, and he would not have succeeded in initiating Word War 2 had he applied that technique. To achieve his goals, he had to master the art of manipulation. With that, he knew he was more dangerous than all the weapons in the world put together. With words and words alone, Hitler damn near put the world to an end. He applied the psychology of manipulation and the result was devastating. The man with the strange mustache, the man of average height and stature, became so powerful that he caused the destruction of cities, the deaths of millions of men, women, and children. He threatened continents, not countries; he declared that he would make Africans fetch waters from the Atlantic Ocean and water his crops in the Sahara Desert. He was a madman, you will agree, but he was also one of the greatest men who ever lived. He discovered his gift and used it well, albeit to an utterly extreme length. But a lot can be learned from this man named Adolf Hitler.

Always have it at the back of your mind that you are not the only person with a mind-frame, other people have their mind-frames, too. And you will come across those who would try to exercise their mind-frame over yours. It now depends on how strong you are; it's a battle of the mind. Will you allow the second party's mind to dominate yours or the other way round? Everything absolutely depends on you and your ultimate choice. Do not be passive in the affair of the mind; passivity will only bring you enslavement. You must always know when someone is trying to exercise his mind-frame over yours. Ignorance of the mind is the worst kind of disease ever. If you are blinded by deception, you can hardly see it when another person is trying to manipulate you. Manipulation is a practice being used today by leaders all around us: religious leaders, political leaders, and community leaders. They trick you into things you will never think of doing had a regular person ask. And because they stand in the throne of leadership, you think they know it all, you think they are the messiahs, but they are not, they are just human beings like you. The only difference might be that they have trained their mind-frames to be so strong that hardly any other mind can best theirs, but they are still fallible, they are still prone to make mistakes even though they present themselves as the most perfect beings and see you as their subordinates. Liberation begins from the mind, my friend. When you begin to see yourself as a leader too, when you begin to train your mind to become as strong and as sharp of these men you admire, then you are on the right path to your freedom of the mind.

This book will build you to become the next Adolf Hitler (in a good way, of course – I am not building you to become a madman that will threaten to cause the end of mankind). You will learn how you can easily manipulate people and cause them to tow your path. Like I already said your mind is like a power-station; it is capable of supplying light to cities as it chooses. Therefore, you can learn the art of mind-control to make other people do your biddings. The human mind is a fragile thing only if you understand how to manipulate it effectively. There are people whose minds are begging to be controlled, to be manipulated; they need people to tell them how to live, how to breathe, what to eat, what job to apply for. This is where you take absolute control of them. This book will also teach you how to take advantage of people's emotional weaknesses and then ultimately brainwash them.

The methods in this book may seem crude but they are very necessary for the man who wants to master the art of dark psychology.

1

WHAT IS DARK PSYCHOLOGY?

While Psychology is the study of human behavior, and such study is centered on our thoughts, actions, and interactions, Dark Psychology is that phenomenon by which people use the tactics of persuasion, manipulation, coercion, and motivation to get what they want, either morally or immorally. Basically, Dar Psychology is the art and science of human manipulation and mind control to achieve one's desired goals without the victim knowing they are being manipulated.

The true purpose of this book, you should know, is not majorly to lecture you on how to avoid being manipulated and exploited, it is also to remind you of how easily it can be to desire to use the manipulative tactics that will later be explained as you read further. This book will challenge you to assess the necessary tactics you need to understand in various areas of your life such as parenting, leadership, relationship, work, romantic and friendship.

It is true that while people who make use of these tactics know their true intentions and are concerned about manipulating other people to get what they want, there are others who make use of the same dark psychology without knowing that they are doing it. Such kinds of people will consider the application of such manipulative tactics as normal processes and have no idea that it can be evil or immoral. These kinds of people have learned the tactics right from their childhood from their parents, and there are some people who learn it from their teenage years or adulthood basically by chance. They applied the technique unintentionally and it worked for them. Since they got what they wanted through the techniques, they continued to apply the tactics.

There are other cases where some people are trained to make use of these tactics. Training programs that enlighten them about the use of the dark, unethical psychological and persuasion tactics are all around us; the typical sales and marketing programs we come across every day are part of the training programs that lean on the side of the dark psychological methods. A lot of them use dark methods to create a brand or sell a product with the main purpose of their own interests or their companies', not always for the interest of the customers, even though it might appear that way. There are various people who make use of the dark psychological methods in their everyday lives; such people include narcissists, sociopaths, attorneys, politicians, sales personnel, selfish people, amongst others.

Having knowledge of the psychology of human being is akin to being a superman. Sometimes, with your knowledge of how people think and reason, and knowing what their next course of action is going to be, others tend to call you a freak, because you are able to do what they have never imagined possible. But it is all psychology. We usually tend to refer to the term 'psychology' sparsely, in a too weak manner for its credit. Perhaps we have to look deep into its meaning; maybe by doing that we will be able to understand its power. *Psychology is the understanding of the mind of a person and the way it functions.* Psychology, even though its definition in this book may be short, encompasses the existence of all human beings, and it controls advertising, crime, finance, religion, business, love and hate. A person who has a deep understanding of psychology has the power to influence human beings; a power which only a few people hold.

In the bid to differentiate between those motivations that are dark and those that are ethical, you first have to observe your intent. You need to ask yourself if the method you intend to use is aimed at helping other people or hurting them. Morally, in the application of the dark psychological principles on other people, having a mutually beneficial outcome should be the main objective (we shall discuss this in later chapters).

It is a psychological nature for people to prey upon other people for selfish gains. Basically, all of humanity has the potential to victimize other people and living creatures at large. While many people restrain or do away with these tendencies because of their moral view on things, others embrace them and act on these impulses. Dark Psychology is just a manner of trying got to understand these thoughts, feelings, and perceptions that create human predatory behaviors. In the next century, the predatory nature of most human beings on the internet would have spun out of control; internet predators and their acts of violence, theft, and abuse will become a societal epidemic, or global phenomenon, if not controlled. These predatory behaviors include such vices like cyberterrorism, cyberbullying, cyberstalking, cybercrimes, online sexual predatory and political or religious fanaticism will be engaged in cyber warfare.

The concept of Dark Psychology studies both criminal and deviant behavior and a framework for discovering the potential for committing evil within the human psyche. The psychological nature of people to act in a predatory manner upon others is motivated by criminal or deviant drives that that lack purpose and general assumption of instinctual drives and social sciences theory.

The position of the Dark Psychology is the revelation that all human being possess the reservoir of malevolent intentions towards other people ranging from minimally obstructive and fleeting thoughts to pure psychopathic deviant behaviors without any cohesive rationality, which can also be referred to as the Dark Continuum. The Dark Psychology covers everything that makes us the kinds of people we are, depending on the kind of relationship we have with our dark side. Every one of us is a moon, and we have that dark side which we never show to anybody. All our culture, faith and humanity have the origin of the Dark Psychology about them.

The more people are knowledgeable about the concept of the Dark Psychology, the less they are likely to fall victim to it. For a human being, it is very important, at least to an extent, to have the basic idea of the Dark Psychology.

Dark Psychology is a universal part of the human condition. Indeed, most benevolent people have the evil of Dark Psychology embedded in them but they have chosen to not act upon it, as it goes against their own dogma of morality and humanity. These people are hardly involved in any form of violence or abuse. In the world of Dark Psychology, all human beings have the potential for violence or abuse, but some people have the right fortitude to suppress their act of violence.

Having a true knowledge of human psychology is such a difficult thing to achieve. The search for true psychology is like the hunt for the Holy Grail; it might seem like a myth but it exists, and only people who have it will be able to use it. And so, to find this elusive concept called psychology a searcher must have to pore through every page of relevant book, must visit crypts and tombs of psychological bones, plow through libraries, differentiate the useful information from the irrelevant. But for the fact that you are reading this book right now, you have to search no further, for you are already at the apex of the search for the truth in the world of psychology. To gain from the abundant knowledge of this book, no special understanding is required of you. The only thing you need is the readiness and willingness to learn and apply this knowledge in practice.

This book exposes some hidden truths which only very few people know its existence or even understand – the truth in the world of 'dark psychology'. These are the tricks used by the most powerful people in the world who have gathered a lot of followers and amassed wealth through the right application of this unique brand of psychology.

You will not only be taught how dark psychology came to be and how it forms an important part of our consciousness, but you will also learn how to apply its principles. In addition to these, some true stories of relevant cases will be given so you can easily understand how the dark psychology has been applied historically and presently.

Understanding Dark Psychology

Dark psychology abounds all around us. When you switch on your television, you see it being displayed, when you go to work, you witness it among your superior and colleagues (even though they might be mildly applied in that case). You may not like what dark psychology stands for, but it's there. Now you have the choice of either accepting or rejecting it. If you choose to remain ignorant of it, then you have chosen to become the victim of dark psychology; but you can choose to learn its intricacies and then know how to defend yourself with this knowledge, especially against those people who are ready to destroy you with their own psychological strength.

Understanding dark psychology is not only for the protection of yourself alone. There are things you can learn that will help you become a better person both personally and professionally. Kill of the idea that people with the knowledge of the dark psychology are madmen; no, but it really does not hurt to have a little power in this world of dog-eat-dog we live in.

The usage of this book is entirely up to you; the understanding of the principles therein is also up to you. This book can be the most powerful method of defense you have ever come across, or it can be your fountain of opportunities. The principles and instances given in this book are basic tools you can use to build the skyscraper of knowledge.

You should be warned beforehand, however, that this book is not for the weak-hearted. If you know you will not be able to deal with the crude principles herein, you better not move on to the next page, for once you flip off the mask and see the face of the clown beneath, there is no going back.

Think deeply about your choice before you go further into the world of dark psychology.

2

THE DARK PERSUASION TECHNIQUES

Almost everyone in the world is familiar with the concept of persuasion, but only a few understand the hidden intricacies of this art. A lot of articles and books have been written to help people become more persuasive. However, there is a difference between mere persuasion and dark persuasion.

The dictionary might say that to persuade another person is to prevail on someone to do or believe something by applying any of the numbers of methods of advising or reasoning. However, the difference between persuasion and dark persuasion is in the intention. A persuader might attempt to convince someone to do something without thinking through specific tactics or motivation or without any real understanding of the person they are trying to persuade. A persuader's intention might be in creating the most good for the people they are trying to persuade. An example is a diplomat whose mission is to prevent war between two world powers by creating political ties where there were previously none. A persuader might try to grasp at straws wildly hoping for something to stick.

Persuasion is the attempt to get someone to do something you want. Not all persuasions are dark persuasions. There are various persuasion techniques that are different from the conventional dark psychology. If a negotiator talks to some suicide bombers to shed off their vest then persuasion has taken place. This kind of persuasion, with a positive and generally acceptable result, is known as the positive persuasion. However, there is no denying the fact that there is dark persuasion.

What sets the positive persuasion apart from the negative is the motive. Positive persuasion is applied to encourage someone to do something that would not injure or harm them. Positive persuasion can save lives, and a lot of people agree with this type of persuasion, of course. The intention of a dark persuader, however, is a lot different.

A dark persuader usually understands the bigger picture. He understands who he is trying to persuade, what motivates them, and how far he needs to take the tactics in order to be successful. He is typically unconcerned with the morality of his manipulation. He might see "doing the right thing" as a perk, but it doesn't have to be his biggest motivation.

Dark persuasion is devoid of any form of morality. If positive persuasion is a way of helping people help themselves, then the concept of the dark persuasion is making the victims do something again their self-interest. In some occasion, the victims may take the wrong steps begrudgingly because they know they are not doing the right thing, but they have no choice or they just want to stop the relentless persuasion from the manipulator.

In the Venn diagram of morality and self-gratification, a dark persuader's action will not always fall into the overlapping area. A dark persuader will see the thing or person he wants and devise a way to get it by any means.

The motives of dark persuaders vary according to the individual manipulator. Some manipulators attempt to persuade people to do a thing to their own benefits, while other persuaders do theirs with the wicked intention of causing harm to their victims.

The result of dark persuasion is also quite different from that of the positive persuasion. The positive persuasion usually results in any of the following three scenarios: advantage to the person being persuaded, an advantage to both the persuader and the persuaded, or a benefit for the persuaded and a person different from the persuader. Basically, positive persuasion often results in the benefit of the persuaded, too. There is usually no situation of a positive persuasion where the persuasion benefits only the persuader, which is often the case of a dark persuader, in which they benefit, either directly or indirectly.

In the case of the dark persuasion, the person being persuaded goes against what they believe in and they do not benefit from the persuasion. The most experienced persuaders usually not only benefit by harming their victims in the course of the persuasion, but they also harm third parties. An example is the case of a dark persuader who talks a person into committing suicide simply because he has something to gain from the death of the victim. In this instance, the persuader will gain from the death of the victim but the victim has lost their life, and their death has hurt the people who cared about them.

Dark persuaders have characteristics that reveal the traits of their identities. They are often indifferent to the outcome of their actions, and they lack the ability to care about how their persuasions might affect the lives of other people. Such kinds of persuaders usually reveal narcissistic traits or they view their own need as a lot more important than other people's needs. Some can be sociopathic and thus unable to understand the concept of another person's emotion.

There are various instances of dark persuasion. Most of the toxic relationships we witness all around us could be the result of dark persuasion. One partner in a relationship may be trying to persuade the other. In some weird cases, however, both partners darkly persuade each other. Such an attempt of persuasion can be enduring, and the relationship eventually becomes psychologically abusive. A partner may forbid another from taking a new and better job or pursuing their childhood dreams. The dark persuader may hide under the cloak of convincing the victim of acting for the good of the relationship, but the persuader is only hurting both themselves and the relationship itself.

Some people may debate the reality of the dark persuasion; they may doubt that it really exists, but any doubt they may have can make them easy prey to the reality of the persuasion itself. They often fall victim to skilled manipulators, and they will continue doubting until things really get out of hand. Expert persuaders often apply tactics to benefit themselves in the long run.

This method of persuasion is often slow and requires a lot of patience from the persuader, for it rarely brings about the instant result. Some people are able to resist being persuaded because they feel like they are being pressured, or the lack the trust or close relationship with the person who is trying to persuade them. The long con, however, is able to defeat any of these challenges because it requires the right time for manifestation.

In this kind of persuasion, the persuader takes their time to gain their victim's trust. They will make sure their victim likes and then trusts them enough. As soon as the victim has been prepared enough for the slaughterhouse, the persuader begins the psychological warfare against their target. Most times, they begin with some false positive persuasion. The persuader will manipulate their victim into taking some steps or making some choices, that are for their own advantage. This has two purposes, actually. One, the victim becomes accustomed to being persuaded by the persuader and so does not question the motive when the dark persuasion is thus presented. The victim makes a mental connection between the persuader and the positive result; in this manner, even if the victim is presented with the dark persuasion, they would ultimately expect something positive to come from it.

Usually, dark persuaders (the skilled ones) carry out their persuasions stealthily. They search for the perfect victim and set to work. Skilled persuaders do not just try to darkly persuade everyone they come across. They must pick their victims and start building the trust right from the foundation.

Let us consider the situation of a widowed woman who is desperate and vulnerable due to her age and bereavement. She is befriended by a man who is either an old friend or a church member. The man starts working out his persuasion after some time. He gives the lady the illusion that he truly cares about her. He shows her kindness, care and he is absolutely romantic to her. After some time, her guard drops when she is around him.

This man starts by carrying out some small acts of positive persuasion, like advising her of ways to make sure that her monthly bills are reduced. The woman appreciates these little efforts and becomes submissive to him; she takes his advice without considering the negative implication that might surface. Ordinarily, she wouldn't have accepted such advice had she not have an emotional attachment with the man. But because the man has proven to be trustworthy to her, she loses her guard. As soon as her guard is entirely down, the man darkly persuades her to let him help her invest some of her money. Of course, she trustingly obliges. The man, the dark persuader, the manipulator, takes everything he can from her. If he is skilled enough, the lady will not blame him for the 'loss' of the money. She will end up feeling as though the man truly tried to help her but only had bad luck. Dark persuasion can be as deep as that.

Whenever people hear about some bizarre acts of dark persuasion, they tend to question the reality of such actions. In cases where they hear about some people being talked into suicide or murder, it often seems to them incredible, unbelievable. Who would agree to do such a thing? But these doubters do not realize that dark persuasion is not always the out-of-the-blue request. Dark persuasion should be seen as a staircase into the lair of the absurd. The persuader will influence the victim into taking one step at a time. Of course, this does not seem like something serious until things blow out of proportion for the unaware victim. Before they realize it, they are a long way down to the foot of the staircase and the persuader will not allow them any step up again.

An example of the graduality process is a case of a psychopathic criminal that wants other people to commit crimes for them. But if you cannot imagine such kind of person, imagine the gang bosses, cult leaders, or indeed

Charles Mason. This psychopath would not start by asking people to murder just suddenly. They may begin by committing little crimes or hiding a weapon for their persuader. But in time, the crimes the persuaders lure their victims to commit get increasingly severe. From hiding weapons, the victims begin to use the weapons, and it only goes up from there. The persuader often has the wisdom to hold these little crimes over their victims, and before the victims know it they are neck-deep in the crime. They can, therefore, easily be persuaded into committing some more shocking crimes because, to them, they have no choice.

Skilled persuaders rely on the power of graduality to increase the gravity of the persuasion they have over their victims.

Persuaders have several methods of using dark psychological principles to get what they desired. Disguising one's intention is an important step in carrying out a brilliant dark persuasion. Skilled persuaders can employ the various approaches in different manners, depending on the kind of victim they have.

Best persuaders have been able to make use of a dark principle that reveals that people often find it difficult to refuse two simultaneous requests. For instance, a dark persuader may want to take $100 from a victim without the intention of paying. Such a wise manipulator may start by explaining why they need a loan of $1000 and further explaining the terrible consequence that may happen if such loan is not taken. The unknowing victim, however, may feel a sense of compassion or guilt towards the manipulator and wish they could be of assistance. They, of course, will say $1000 is too large for them to lend out. The persuader will then bring down the amount to $200 (which they actually wanted). This time around, they will have a reason, like saying the $200 will still keep them afloat for a couple of days. The victim feels too awkward and becomes unable to refuse this second request. The persuader will end up getting the money they had initially set out to get and the victim will not know what hit them, or how such an amount was taken from them so easily.

Another way of hiding one's true intention is by the application of reverse psychology. Some people have 'boomerang' personality. These kinds of people are naturally wired to refuse to go to a direction they are thrown, and instead will tow the opposite paths.

If a dark persuader is able to identify someone with a boomerang personality, then they have identified a chink in the person's armor. For instance, a persuader has a friend who is in love with a girl that is undecided about choosing a friend or a third party. He knows, however, that this friend will use the girl and then dump her; and that is exactly what the dark persuader wants. If the persuader recognizes the girl as one with a boomerang character, he will try to talk the girl into going for the third party who will treat her well. But he knows that the girl will choose his friend who will treat her bad over the third party that will treat her kindly.

Verbal persuasion is a very effective tool for a dark persuader, and one of the most important methods of a verbal persuader is the application of leading questions in getting what they want. Leading questions are those questions particularly asked to trigger a certain kind of response in their victims. In an instance, a leading persuader may ask their targeted victim such question as "so how bad do you think those people are?" The question, of course, implies that the people he is asking about are definitely bad, but to a certain degree, and the persuader wants the target to give their own assessment of the degree of badness. That kind of question contrasts directly with such non-leading questions as "how do you feel about those people?"

Skilled dark persuaders use leading questions very carefully. If the victim begins to think that they are being led, they will naturally resist and become hard to persuade. A persuader who becomes aware of what is happening (like the leading question is not producing the desired result) they will switch methods immediately, and only return to the leading question when the victim is calm and relaxed.

State outlines the general mood of a person in a particular situation. If someone is aligned in their thoughts, words, and actions, then this shows an example of a strong congruent state. The principle of state transference involves a situation where someone with a better state [of mind] is able to transfer their emotional state to another with a weaker state. This concept is powerful when it is used by a skilled persuader.

A person trying to carry out persuasion, and is aware of the principle that guides state transference, will be able to apply the right technique on the level of control they have over their victim. If the victim is sad and talking slowly, the persuader will channel his own state into this level of lachrymose. By doing so, they create a feeling of trust and rapport on a deep level with their target.

After a leveled match between the persuader and the target, the persuader will begin to cleverly alter their own state to determine how compliant the target would be. For instance, the persuader may slightly speed up their tone of voice to determine whether the target will match their own pace. If the target shows any sign of compliance with this increased state, then this is a sign that the persuader has reached the point of the hook.

Once the point of hook has been ascertained, the persuader will alter their own state to whichever one they want their victim to possess. This, however, could be a happy and positive state, or angry and sad state, depending on which state exactly is going to benefit the dark persuader at the time. This method shows the impression of the subconscious ideas on the success or failure of any given persuasion.

Dark or not, there are various persuasion techniques a person can always employ when the occasion arises. We shall be observing some of these techniques.

The 'Even If' Technique

Almost everyone believes that they are special; they believe, within themselves, that they are above average. This conception is so well supported in the field of psychology that it has half a dozen names: the illusory superiority, the above-average effect, the superiority bias, the leniency error, and the primus inter pares effect. All these describe the same thing – that most people believe they are better than other people.

The fictional town of "Lake Wobegon" was created to talk about this effect. It is a magical place where "all the women are strong, all the men are good looking, and all the children are above average." What does this have to do with persuasion? If people think they are special and above average, why should they think your persuasion will work on them? What you need to do is start addressing a person's objections before they even have a chance to think them.

Your prospect feels like you can read their mind – and that what you are actually proposing can solve their problems.

The 'Because...' Technique

Imagine you're waiting in line at an ATM, trying to withdraw some money. I walk up to you and ask: "Can I cut in front of you?"

What would you do?

Depending on your mood, you might have some choice words to send my way. You might politely decline. You might let me go ahead just because of how taken aback you are by the weird request.

Now imagine that I instead said this: "Can I cut in front of you because I'm in a rush?"

Maybe your withdrawal is not as urgent, or you just feel like being nice. You might not always let me cut in front, but this is better than my first (quite rude) question.

However, what if I said, "Can I cut in front of you because I need to withdraw some money?"

What would you do then? I'll let you think about it. Researchers have studied this question.

94% of people waiting in line let the person in a rush cut in front of them.

Shockingly, 93% let people cut in front of them "because they needed to withdraw some money."

"Because I need to withdraw some money" is a meaningless statement – that's the only reason, technically speaking, why anyone ever needs to use the ATM.

The reason for the huge jump in cutting (only 60% let themselves be cut in the first condition) is the word "because." The word "because" is powerful. It gives people a reason to believe what you say. Apply it in your interaction to make your communication more persuasive.

Anticipation

In three days, you're going to make out with a celebrity of your choice. Or you can do it right now. Which do you pick? There is research about this. behavioral economist George Loewenstein asked people how much they are willing to pay to kiss a celebrity of their choice.

Amazingly, people were willing to pay the most money to kiss a celebrity in three days – even though "right now" was also an option.

The reason for this, since supported in a variety of other, less absurd studies, is anticipation. The excitement leading up to something is as important – and in some cases more important – than the thing itself.

How can you use this to your advantage? Build excitements for your intention. Say that something big is coming and what it will help people do – but don't tell them what it is. Build excitement. Use anticipation.

Foot-in-the-door Technique

In his autobiography, Benjamin Franklin wrote that "He that has once done your kindness will be more ready to do you another, than he whom yourself have obliged." This observation has been called the "Ben Franklin effect," and was the inspiration for a series of psychology studies that led to the discovery of the "foot-in-the-door technique", or FITD for short.

FITD was first studied by Stanford psychologists Jonathan Freedman and Scott Fraser in 1966. Freedman and Fraser wanted to test Franklin's idea: that someone will agree to a larger request after they have first agreed to a smaller one.

The researcher called on houses in California. For some houses, they asked if the people would mind a large, obtrusive road sign being planted in their front yard. Unsurprising, this was not a popular idea.

For other houses, they first asked whether the house would be willing to display a much smaller, unobtrusive sign. The sign was quite unobjectionable, so many people said yes.

Interestingly, when houses displaying the small sign were asked if they were willing to display the big, ugly sign *more said yes*. Someone who has agreed to a small request is more likely to agree to a large request later.

The Door-in-the-face Technique

The foot-in-the-door technique gets more people to agree to a large request by first asking a small request. What if you did it the other way around? The door-in-the-face technique is asking an excessively large request (which gets declined) before a more reasonable request makes people more likely to agree with the reasonable request.

In classic research carried out on this technique, researchers asked people to mentor juvenile delinquents two hours a week for two years. Unsurprisingly, not many people agreed to do that. Even if it were you being requested, would you agree? Some people were then asked if they would be willing to help bring the juvenile delinquents to the zoo, a one-day task.

Does making a large request before a small request actually work? People who were only asked to chaperone the day trip said yes 17% of the time. But people who were first asked mentor delinquents for 2 years said yes to the smaller request 50% of the time.

The door-in-the-face technique is very powerful and effective. How do you use this to your advantage? Downplay your intention. First, make a ridiculously high request, then make the smaller one after the first has been rejected.

3

COVERT MANIPULATION METHOD

The devil is in the detail. Many dark psychological tricks, tactics and principles make use of the covert manipulation method. Therefore, to go further into the dark world of psychological manipulation, we have to get a full understanding of the covert manipulation method. As you learn further about the underground world of dark psychology and its impacts, you will be able to identify the signs of covert manipulation. Understanding what the covert manipulation stands for is the first process of the knowledge of the dark psychology.

The sophisticated shallow charming persona of the psychopath whitewashes over the sinister tactics that actually operate their day to day lives: the covert (some unconscious) manipulation of the truth, the target's emotions, other people's perceptions of the target and themselves. The things they do for their self-gratification and aggrandizement, counter to what they say to win hearts and minds.

Our focus here is on the smooth-talking glib easy-going charming person-magnet. Our focus is on the behavior that no one else can see but those they prey on, or those outside the charmed circle, and few would believe if they could see it anyway.

Covert manipulation method is the attempt of a person to control the thoughts and feelings of another individual in such a hidden way that the person being influenced is unaware of the manipulation being played on him. The word 'covert' itself means the method manipulators use in hiding their true intentions. People who are victims of the covert kind of manipulation usually do not know that that they have been manipulated; they would not understand how the manipulation has been carried out on them, or even be able to ascertain the motives of their manipulators. The covert manipulation method is a dangerous technique, and it avoids being discovered until the damage has already been done. The covert manipulation method can come in various ways, but we are focusing on the emotional part of it. Various other kinds of covert manipulation method include people's beliefs, behaviors, and willpower. Covert emotional manipulation method is channeled on impacting the emotional state and reality of a person. Taking advantage of someone's emotional state of mind and manipulating it is akin to cutting off their jugular vein. A person with emotional control has full control of every aspect of his own life.

An influencer has the mindset of "I will help you make the right decision". But a manipulator's mindset is "I want to secretly control you to my own benefit".

There are four situations in which covert emotional manipulation can be manifested. They include the professional, romantic, personal and family spheres of life. Once you understand the concept of these four kinds of manipulation and their application, you will be able to not only use them to your advantage but also protect yourself against it.

A romantic partner that controls another is a good example of the covert emotional manipulation method. If a person is in a relationship with another person and the partner is trying to control them, the person will most often not like it and will always look for ways to get out of such a toxic relationship. And so because of this, a lot of controlling partners tends to exercise their domination in a covert manner. Their partners become victims of the manipulation without even realizing that they were being manipulated. This makes the partners continue to exercise their domination without the fear of the partner finding out or walking away, as the case may be.

A friend may make use of the emotional manipulation method to get what they want out of the relationship they are in. One of the most familiar types of manipulators is the ones that put in the minds of their friends the feelings of sympathy, compassion, guilt, and obligation towards them. The friend who is being manipulated will be unaware that they are being influenced. They will not be able to explain the way they behave and feel towards their manipulating friends.

The professional sector is also another basis for the emotional manipulation method to manifest. A lot of people have confessed to having worked for a boss or a superior who has triggered in them a feeling of submissiveness, guilt, fear or duty in them. And they usually fail to identify where or why this strange feeling surfaced. The following are some of the undetectable covert manipulation methods.

Hypnotic Charm

The most charismatic person in the room, he focuses the spotlight of his full attention on you. With large doses of direct eye contact, he is totally fascinated by whatever it is you have to say. If he is a celebrity narcissist, he appears utterly fascinated by the story of how you listened to his music/ saw his movie/ watched him play footie when you were a kid, but it will seem as if you were the first person to ever tell him this, and he is utterly flattered and humbled by such a revelation. You walk away proclaiming, "Wow, he is such a nice humble decent down-to-earth guy!" ten minutes after you have met him.

Love Bombing

This is usually employed by manipulators at the beginning of their interaction with their victims. It includes the intense, forceful and sudden exhibition of positive feelings towards the victim. This may initially appear counterintuitive in the first place. If a person is trying to harm another person, why do they act in the person's interest at first? The answer is simple – because it is part of their plans; it serves their original and deeper objective.

Love bombing brings about a feeling of affection, trust and compliance from a victim to their manipulator. The degree of the use of the love bombing and the people it is used against depends widely upon the manipulator's assessment of the situation. A victim who is lonely, desperate, yearns for support and comfort can easily be love bombed more intensely or overtly, depending on how the manipulator thinks they will be receptive to it. It is hard to imagine love bombing as something negative. "This person has always

been nice to me, and I feel good whenever I'm around him."
This kind of statement is a positive one, and it is unlikely to
trigger any feeling of abuse taking place.

Various people respond differently to the loving gesture
showered on them. While some are controlled by gifts,
compliments work well on some other people.

Word Play – Empty or Loaded Words – 'Word Salad'

Practiced yarn-spinners, a manipulator knows exactly
the right words to choose to:

- Put a convincing argument,
- Induce an emotional reaction (flatter, confuse,
  stifle, insult, defuse, inflame), or
- Paint a picture (impress, suggest, plant a seed of
  doubt, build on commonly-held assumptions).

Telling you exactly what you want to hear, they will make
promises, commitments, vows and oaths they have no
intention of fulfilling. "I love you. I've waited my whole life
for you. I've finally met my soulmate. I'll never leave you,"
are utterly easily and frequently (and to many targets over a
lifetime). Over time, you will notice that their pledges and
self-professed image of themselves do not match up with
their actions. They continually break promises, let you down,
are never there for you when you need them.

Masters of the double-entendre, they occasionally utter
words that seem nonsensical or out of place. Because these
utterances are odd, we can let them through to keeper when
in fact they are glimpses of true intention. Expert lie-

detectors call them, "tells". Often in the form of black humor. For example, "we can get married, settle down, have kids and drive each other nuts!", or, "Now we are married darling, it's all downhill from here. ha ha ha".

Reinforcement

Love bombing is the unconditional and positive display from a manipulator to his victim from the beginning of their interaction. The purpose of the love bombing is to soften the defenses of the target, increasing their dependence on the manipulator and ultimately setting up the possibility of a positive relationship or friendship.

Positive reinforcement is the next process after the love bombing. Reinforcement is, therefore, a switch in behavior where the manipulator no longer displays a feeling of positivity towards his victim anymore. Instead, he holds on to that positivity until the victim begins to behave in the way he wants it. For example, if the manipulator wants their victim to visit them often, the manipulator will only show a positive response when this happens. The victim will not be aware that the positive attention is being used in a strategic manner against them, and will therefore subconsciously obey the wishes of the manipulator so as to experience the positive feelings the person offers.

This reinforcement becomes predictable. The victim begins to know that there is a pattern of way the manipulator wants. If what the manipulator is done, the positivity the victim wants is then realized. However, as the positive reinforcement is ascertained, the manipulator goes further to apply the intermittent positive reinforcement (IPR). This means withholding positivity even when the desired behavior has been met. For instance, if the manipulator wants their victims to call them more and the victim complies, the manipulator will only show positivity some of the time, not every time the desired behavior is displayed by the victim.

This unpredictability usually elicits a craving of positive response from the manipulator, without the victim ever having the knowledge of the kind of manipulation going on. The victim will begin to do everything possible to attract a positive reaction from the manipulator. The manipulator will cause their victims behaving in certain ways they want, and the victims will not be aware of the reason they are behaving that way, or how they begin to behave in that way in the first place.

These are simply how the process of love bombing, positive reinforcement, and intermittent positive reinforcement works under the covert manipulation method. However, these three processes can birth the concept of another emotional manipulation known as the reality denial which, basically, has its impact on the mind rather than on the emotions of the victim. The result of the reality denial can shatter a victim's emotion.

Backhanded Compliments

Barbed comments in which a derogatory observation is disguised within an apparent compliment. "You handled that really well, given that you are so weak and sensitive. You did a good job on the books, especially when you are bad with figures. Doesn't this dress make my wife slimmer than she is?"

Belittling

Behavior such as rolling eyes, tut-tutting, taking 'down to', mocking, scoffing or teasing. Demeaning the target's opinions, achievements, and abilities in both a private and public context. Indices or increases low self-esteem. Such a common socially-acceptable male treatment of women in this culture that it flies under the radar for many of us.

The Silent Treatment

Stonewalling, refusing to engage, leaving the room or the home for hours or even days at a time. The target has plenty of time to question what it is they said or did that caused the emotional and physical withdrawal of the manipulator, and becomes conditioned to avoid certain behavior as a result. It becomes patently clear what is "off limits", and important issues slowly becoming a simmering volcano of unspoken concerns underlying day-to-day life.

Reality Denial

It is usually scary for a person to imagine the possibility of losing his own mind, his sanity, his self-identity. And it is usually bad when it is explained by such understandable term as mental illness or the resultant effect of stress. It is more unsettling, however, if that feeling of sanity is hereby induced by a manipulator.

Reality denial is one of the numerous covert manipulation methods that have the same aim, which is shattering a victim's sanity to serve their own selfish interests.

One of the major aims of weakening a victim's sanity is by the application of the graduality process. Wise manipulators rarely aim for the total destruction of their victim's sanity because such a method usually goes undetected. Experienced manipulators rather choose the "slowly but surely" approach; which is the gradual washing off of their victim's sanity until they can hardly believe their own faculties.

Covert manipulators often begin with the small-scale erosion of their victim's confidence by messing with their memory. The manipulators will employ various means of manipulation on their victims in such a way that the victim is left questioning their recollection of happenings. The manipulator will make sure their own account of the event is the one seemingly believable.

The process of reality denial serves two hidden purposes. First, it reduces the victim's trust in their own power of understanding and the recollection of events. Secondly, which is the result of the first, this trust is thus transferred onto the manipulator instead. The victim will now always require the manipulator to do the thinking for him. Of course, this may not seem serious at first.

In time, the covert manipulator will make very important how severe the events they make the victim doubt. What starts as a seemingly harmless and insignificant technique will eventually burst up into a victim losing all the confidence in their own thought process. The most dangerous and sure element is to make the victim blame their own mind for the loss of the remembrance ability. Experienced manipulators will be pulling the emotional string without letting the victim aware of what is really going on.

Hurried Intimacy

He progresses the relationship quickly to sharing his innermost insecurities desires ambitions and 'shame' in an effort to have you reciprocate. When you do, as is natural, he will later use his knowledge of your intimate secrets as a tool to control and manipulate you. Quick to move into your home. Quick to talk about a shared future. Quick to propose marriage. "Whirlwind romance".

Lying

A covert emotional manipulator outrightly lies while looking you straight in the eye. There are huge omissions that leave holes in the jigsaw, over time, you will find you have an increasing pile of jigsaw pieces that don't fit into the picture he has painted. Another method of their falsehood is the twisted truths. Embellished truths – a tiny truth at the center of a Russian Doll wrapped in layers of lies.

4

WHAT IS THE DARK TRIAD?

S ome people have personality traits that can make it disagreeable or difficult to deal with them. They may be volatile, arrogant, or domineering, but, with careful management, you can develop their strengths, neutralize the unsavory elements of their behavior, and restore team harmony.

But some other behaviors and characteristics can be seriously damaging and, if someone displays a toxic combination of these traits, he can undermine his colleagues in a lasting way, and he can potentially poison and destroy a team.

The Dark Triad is a phrase you're likely to have heard around the workplace, but it is one of the buzzwords in the world of psychology.

The Dark Triad is basically the identification of the three most dangerous psychological traits a person can possess. The Dark Triad is just like a fountain where every other form of the dark psychology stems. These three destructive traits are Narcissism, Psychopathy, and Machiavellianism.

Narcissism

Narcissism comes from the Greek myth of Narcissus, a hunter who fell in love with his own reflection in a pool of water and drowned. Narcissistic people can be selfish, boastful, arrogant, lacking in empathy, and hypersensitive to criticism.

Generally, people believe narcissism means the act of overly loving oneself. A narcissist is considered as a person with an over bloated self-esteem who sees himself as superior to other people. In essence, however, one can have self-love without being a narcissist. A person who meets the medical diagnostic criteria for narcissism to a level of having psychological disorder often exhibits the traits of the Dark Triad. The mind of a narcissist is so dark that he sees himself as the better species of human being and others are meant to serve him. Their behavior often shows their level of self-worth. A narcissist will never accept criticism or anyone have a different opinion from theirs. Instead, they enjoy being flattered or praised. They want to be worshipped and constantly given approval and recognition, and they live all their lives in the struggle to maintain such standard.

Psychopathy

Personality traits associated with psychopathy include a lack of empathy or remorse, antisocial behavior, and being manipulative and volatile. It's important to note that there is a distinction between psychopathic traits and being a psychopath, with its commonly held association with criminal violence.

Psychopathy is a mental disorder that borders on the superficial charm, impulsivity and the lack of such emotions as empathy and remorse. A psychopath does not feel sorry for people, and they do not feel any sense of remorse for whatever wrongdoing they may have committed. They live in their own personal world where the distinction between the right and the wrong is measured only by themselves alone. Therefore, what a psychopath sees as the right and normal thing may be considered a horrible thing by other people. Psychopaths are some of the most dangerous people in the world, and they are like wolves in sheep's clothing. Many psychopaths look as sane as any other human being but their level of sanity is far apart from the common man's. The real psychopaths of the world are likely to be the handsome and charming strangers who win their victims over by acting in the most loving ways and eventually end up ruining the lives of their targets; they might even kill their victims instead, which is often the case.

Some of the popular names in businesses have psychopathic tendencies; for psychopaths are known to get to the peak of any field they choose, the height of power; and when they attain that height, there is usually nothing they cannot do, most times getting away with their acts. Psychopaths delight in seeing other people suffer, and they are not held back by conscience or any feeling of remorse.

Machiavellianism

The word comes from the renowned 16th Century Italian politician and diplomat Niccolo Machiavelli. He earned notoriety when his 1513 book, "The Prince", was interpreted as an endorsement of the dark arts of cunning and deceit in diplomacy. Traits associated with Machiavellianism include duplicity, manipulation, self-interest, and a lack of both emotion and morality.

The origin of this name is traced to the name of the political philosopher Machiavelli. Machiavellianism is the willingness to focus on self-interest at all times; the desire to always look after oneself first above any other people. Others might call it being selfish but it is what it is. Machiavellianism explores the ruthless exercise of cruelty and power over mercy and compassion. Machiavellianism people are very smart; they are incredibly strategic in their approach to life, and when anything or anyone does not meet their level of strategic expectation, they discard such person or thing without giving consideration to the suffering their actions might bring to their victims. Skilled Machiavellianism people are not publicly brutal in their approach, they are instead stealth. They are clever enough to do things that personally serve their own interest while still maintaining a positive public image. This is why it is always hard to identify the real with the Machiavellianism traits in them. They usually find the perfect excuse for whatever step they have taken. Former President Bill Clinton is an example of someone with the Machiavellianism traits. He had extra-marital affairs while still in office and he still managed to be publicly liked regardless of what he did, as a contrast to other political leaders who have done the same and got their career ruined in the process.

The Application Of The Dark Triad

Narcissistic Actions

Many narcissists have had childhood fantasies of being followed and worshipped by a large group of people; and as they grow up, they tend to work towards making those dreams come true, feeling that being worshipped or praised is their destiny. And when they encounter people who do not feel the need to praise them, the narcissists consider their actions as an affront. They take these unyielding people as their worst enemies and will find a way to either make these enemies submit to them or they find a permanent solution to the 'cockroaches' by stamping upon them hard.

The huge self-worth that narcissists experience inwardly is usually reflected on their outward appearances and reactions. They are wired in two different perceptions – the need to be praised and worshipped by other people and the hatred of criticism, rejection or objection. It must always be the ways of the narcissist that must be applied. Being worshipped is as important to them as the air they breathe, and their hatred for criticism is like poison.

Psychopathic Actions

Psychopaths are usually very hard to identify, except by well-trained psychotherapists, because they look like regular human beings like others, and their behaviors in public are often acceptable, even worthy of emulation. However, by carefully studying the outward but inconspicuous manifestation of psychopathy by these people, you will be able to identify them, or at least suspect them, of having psychopathic traits.

Having charm is one outward behavior of someone with psychopathic traits. This kind of charm is often not the deep and genuine one, it is a fake one, superficial. Psychopaths display all the outward signs of charm like physical attractiveness and interest in other people. They use charm as a part of their tools to lure their victims closer. They know that people are most likely capable of lowering their guards to people who display charming characteristics to them, and so they act in a charming manner towards their targets. Whatever charm a psychopath display is only calculated and planned, it is never inherent. Indeed, psychopaths do not have that positive quality of charm about them; instead, they act it out because it is going to bring them the result they want.

Lying, also, is a feature of the psychopathic. Lying alone does not indicate that a person is a psychopath; but when it is combined with other traits, then it becomes a psychopathic personality. A psychopath who does not lie is not really a psychopath. Lying is one of the strongest tools a psychopath can use. Lying comes as naturally to a psychopath as breathing does; psychopaths are irremediable liars, and they are so skilled in the art of falsehood that their victims can hardly tell that they are lying.

A psychopath has no remorse. They are so fueled by their desire to achieve their goal that there is no line they are not willing to cross; and in the course of crossing that line, they have to time to give rein to remorse. They lock their conscience deep down in the crypt of their minds that they feel no shame or guilt for their action, even if they are caught. A normal person who has committed such terrible crime as murder usually feel so overwhelmingly guilty that some of them resort to suicide to relieve themselves of this feeling. But that is not the case of a psychopath who revels in their action and seeks to do more because they feed off that feeling of crime. Asking a psychopath t feel bad for what they have done is like asking a blind man to drive a car on the highway. A psychopath does not feel guilty because the concept of right and wrong is alien to them; what they believe in instead is what is necessary or not, what is useful or not useful; there is no limit to what they can do when they consider it useful. It does not matter to them if it is wrong, a sin or a crime. The only way a psychopath may feel guilty or remorseful is if they are unable to carry out their psychopathic intentions to the satisfactory level they want, or they are caught before they are able to commit the deed. In this case, they may feel bad because they will believe they have let themselves down. But thinking a psychopath will feel bad for what they have done to other things, animals or people is just preposterous.

A lack of control is another feature of a psychopath. Unlike normal human beings who can exercise control over taking some steps. A man whose wife is constantly nagging and cursing him in the home may restrain himself from beating the woman, but that is not the case of a psychopath. If a psychopath feels it necessary to shut her up, he will not hesitate for a moment to carry out the act. He can slap her if it is going to keep the wife from further complaining; however, he will feel no qualm or hesitation in killing her downright if his intention is to shut her up for good. And having done that, he will not feel bad for his action whatsoever; instead, he will revel in the calmness the death of his wife brings him, then move on with his own life without thinking for a moment about the consequence of his own action. That is how the mind of a psychopath is wired. Psychopaths see opportunities and take advantage of such opportunities without any slightest trace of hesitation. Such an opportunity can be killing someone they want to kill, stealing something they wish to steal or raping someone they wish to rape. It is this total lack of hesitation that makes psychopathic people very effective in the military as they will have no hesitation in carrying out assignments. In the world of business also, psychopaths tend to thrive because of the ruthless impulse they possess. The lack of necessary impulse is detrimental to people's progress in life, psychopathically or not.

Psychopaths are also incapable of such feeling as empathy. A psychopath is incapable of feeling sorry or bad for other people, especially if such people are in pain. Rather than feeling bad for them, psychopaths are fascinated by the kind of pains those people are suffering, and if they could worsen the person's situation, they would. A psychopath enjoys seeing the life drain from the eyes of either animal or human beings. Whenever a psychopath sees something bad happen to another person, the first reaction in their mind is wondering how the tragedy can benefit them or how they can use the tragedy to their own sick advantage. Anyone seeking a kind of humanity or compassion from a psychopath is doing nothing but pouring water in a basket and expecting such a basket to be filled to the brim in no time. Psychopathic criminals need to be isolated from people because their brains are wired to always find pleasure in causing pain.

Machiavellian Actions

A Machiavellian person is a political personality who is concerned with maintaining a positive public image even though their actions and decisions are in contrast. They make the public believe that they are worthy of being followed, of being taken as a role model, whereas secretly their intentions are full of vice. Because Machiavellian people are skilled at hiding their behaviors, they are often very hard to recognize; even sometimes when they are pointed out for committing some grievous deeds, the public finds it hard to believe they are capable of doing those things they are accused of, and so they turn their hatred on the accusers, calling them liars and ones seeking cheap publicity. To this day, the positive legacy of Michael Jackson still lives on even after his death, considering how many allegations had been placed on him. Rather than being shunned by the public for the accusations placed against a Machiavellian person, they are liked more because from the accusations, they have been able to elicit a feeling of pity from the general public. These are some of the tactics of skilled Machiavellian people. The public personality of a Machiavellian person is merely a polished image of who they actually are inwardly, and if people could see past this public portrayal of false sainthood, it would be easy to identify what they truly are. Such a process of identification, however, is close to impossible.

Machiavellian people know who they truly are and also how the public see them. This knowledge makes them dangerous and, perhaps, invulnerable to discovery. They understand that they only have to continue maintaining their public image and there is hardly a way they would be discovered, even if they are accused by their victims in the long run. They understand the psychology of the people who follow and place them in high esteem. There are mass murderers who have gotten away with their crimes for a long time because the public's perception about them is entirely different from what people think a murderer is supposed to be. Take a situation of a religious leader who is known for their charity work and kindness towards other people in public whereas they actually commit terrible acts of violence and sexual assault in secret. For a long time, people will never suspect such people of anything bad because the public image is a mask that has covered their true self from people. Real Machiavellian people inspire love and fear in the mind of people who follow them, but they do it in such a way that the fear is not imposed as much as love is. But it has been built in the mind of the follower to both fear and loves the schemer.

Sadism

Although sadism is a concept different from Machiavellianism, Psychopathy, and Narcissism, it also carries a major influence in the Dark Triad; this time, it could be termed the tetrad where the fourth element Sadism is being introduced to the other three elements. Sadism is one of the darkest traits to understand because it is very hard to associate it with people, especially well-standing people of the public.

Sadism is the act of deriving pleasure from other people's pains. A sadist will rather want to see a man in agony that winning the lottery. It is a very sick part of dark psychology. For instance, if a Machiavellian person causes the suffering of another person, they will not regret it, of course, but that does not mean that they will enjoy it either, but if the same person has the sadism trait, they will derive pleasure from the suffering that another person is experiencing, and they will ultimately seek to cause more suffering in the same person, or other people as the case may be. What makes sadism so worryingly special is the fact that the cruelty carried out is for no other reason but pleasure. A sadistic child will chop off a watermelon with savagery because he is imagining the red inside of the fruit to be human flesh. He will derive pleasure in thinking he is killing a human being. Sadists search for the suffering of other people because they are bored and want to be entertained. There are people who pay large amounts of money just to see people get killed.

Identifying The Dark Triad Traits

Traditionally, psychologists have identified Dark Triad traits by measuring different personality types separately.

However, in 2010, Dr. Peter Jonason, then assistant professor of psychology at the University of Western Florida, and his co-author, Gregory Webster, assistant professor of psychology at the University of Florida, developed the "Dirty Dozen" rating scale, or a 12-item methodology, to measure Dark Triad traits.

Jonason and Webster's measure asks people to rate themselves against these questions:

- I tend to manipulate others to get my way.
- I have used deceit or lied to get my way.
- I have used flattery to get my way.
- I tend to exploit others towards my own end.
- I tend to lack remorse.
- I tend to not be too concerned with morality or the morality of my actions.
- I tend to be callous and insensitive.
- I tend to be cynical.
- I tend to want others to admire me.
- I tend to want others to pay attention to me.
- I tend to seek prestige or status.
- I tend to expect special favors from others.

At its basic level, an individual would be rated from, for example, one to seven on each of the 12 tests, giving a possible score of 12 to 84. The higher the score, the higher the probability of having Dark Triad tendencies.

Managing People With Dark Triad Traits

If you believe a member of your team is exhibiting Dark Triad personality traits, what can you do about it? This is a complex area and there are no easy answers. Experienced psychologists stress that there are many subtleties and gradations of personality types, and the behaviors associated with them can change from day today. But as a manager, you will need to address negative behaviors to maintain harmony and productivity within your team.

Spotting Manipulators

There are many positive ways to influence people. Praise and encouragement can inspire a team member to be even more productive, for example. But if someone has more Machiavellian tendencies, he could try to influence co-workers by selfishly manipulating them, perhaps through coercion or deception.

Manipulative people are often good at hiding their behavior or actions, but there are signs you can look out for, such as someone who won't take no for an answer, who always excuses her hurtful behavior, or present a different "face" to different people to serve her purpose.

If you challenge a manipulative person, be specific about what actions you have spotted and how he is harming your team. Make it clear that his behavior must change, and consider performance agreements to hold him accountable.

The Impact Of Dark Triad Traits at Work

It is difficult to find anything positive to say about the impact Dark Triad traits would have in the workplace. Someone with such a psychological makeup would probably display an undesirable behavior, such as being aggressive, volatile, selfish, and deceitful, or a combination of such traits.

A study specifically looking at the Dark Triad at work claims that employees with its character traits are "toxic". In some instances, they lead men, in particular, to be more aggressive in workplace relationships or try to influence people or events more forcefully.

There is evidence that narcissism, at least initially, can come across in relatively positive, desirable ways. A narcissist will often make an effort with her appearance and seem to be charming and friendly. She may well be conscientious and achievement-oriented – as that will also reflect well on her. But in time, her constant "me meme" tendency may become wearing on people around her.

The Dark Triad personality traits can be toxic and damaging in the workplace. But be aware that someone exhibiting these traits may initially be a high achiever and potentially charming, conscientious and achievement-oriented.

There are tools for identifying Dark Triad traits, but it is important to recognize that, unless you are also a skilled psychologist, you should not make a diagnosis on your own. If you do have any concerns about a team member's negative behaviors, you should raise them with your HR department. Your responsibility is to manage the impact of negative behaviors in the workplace, rather than try to diagnose and pin a psychological label on someone.

Conflict management, assertiveness, and emotional intelligence skills will all be useful in managing someone with Dark Triad personality traits before they cause serious damage.

5

DECEPTION TACTICS

Everyone knows that whenever deception is mentioned, there is often a bad intention behind it. Deception is an important branch of dark psychology. Many people have succeeded in confusing lying for deception, but these two are mutually exclusive. Lying is a form of deception, but deception does not border on lies alone. Instead of regarding deception as lies, it is better to consider it a misleading act. Any action that is capable of making someone believe something to be the truth even when it is not can be regarded as deception.

Examples of deception include fraudulently providing evidence for untruth, lying, implying falsehood or omitting the truth. However, not all actions of deception are instances of dark psychology. To some extent, everyone practice deception one way or another. Some people may deceive other people for some reasons like a feeling of inadequacy, embarrassment or even kindness. Studies have shown that most men are prone to lie about their height on dating websites. This, of course, does not mean they are practicing dark psychology. The concept of dark psychology is more severe than that. Some people go as far as making deception about their health, happiness, and ambition. Such examples of deception, too, are not equivalent to the dark psychology form of deception.

Deception can be dark when it is carried out with a negative impression and total disregard for the feeling of the person being deceived. People who make use of the dark psychology deploy the deception with the sole purpose of harming their victims, not to help them. They do it in favor of their own interest regardless of who gets hurt in the process.

Some people think that small-scale deceptions cannot be considered dark where large-scale deceptions are nothing but dark; these people are greatly mistaken. It is not the size, or even the gravity of the deception, that determines whether deception is dark or not; instead, it is the motive behind such deception that measures its state of darkness.

The Spectrum Of Deception

Distributed deception platforms have grown well beyond basic honeypot trapping techniques and are designed for high-interaction deceptions, early detection, and analysis of attackers' lateral movement. Additionally, deception platforms change the asymmetry of an attack by giving security teams the upper hand when a threat enters their network and forcing the attackers to be right 100% of the time or have their presence revealed, and by providing decoys that obfuscate the attack surface and through valuable threat intelligence and counterintelligence that is required to outmaneuver the advanced human attacker.

Small deceptions can be used in a powerfully dark way by a great manipulator, and the resultant effect is often very brutal than the large-scale forms of deception. Small deceptions are often applied to test the victim's level of gullibility and then make them believe the deceptive statements and actions of the manipulator. If people are wired by the manipulator to believe a range of smaller falsehood, they are likely to fall for larger ones over time.

Small deceptions can also be carried out to make ineffective the victim's belief in their powers of logical intuitions. If a manipulator tries to deceive a victim over small deceptions and the victim begins to question what is going on, they begin to conclude that their suspicion is wrong and that they can no longer trust their own judgment. Most people are more prone to conclude that their own judgment is wrong rather than another person ending up deceiving them over less serious issues. The brutal users of dark psychology are not unaware of this trust that people have and they take advantage of it without any form of mercy or the regard for the wellbeing of their victim.

Deception in the large scale can also give sure hint into the dark psychology. One of the deceptions that have always worked is to convince another person that you a different person than you claim to be. This is not in the area of personality or behavior. This time, you are talking about your entire identity. Your name, your birth date, if possible, your sex – everything! The most experienced user of dark psychology often tries to persuade people to believe their false identity and background.

Money is often the basis of most deceptions since deception and money have been known to cross paths a lot of times in the past. People apply deception to attain money while others deceive to conceal their own money, or the lack thereof. Since money is a common topic in the world of deception, a few of its deceptive applications will, therefore, be explored.

One of the most common dark psychology deceptions that involve money is exhibited by the beggars. These are not the regular street beggars; these particular beggars aim to take away money from the public even though they already have plenty of it. These beggars apply a number of dark psychological principles to extract money from innocent victims. Such kinds of beggars are not afraid of inflicting injuries on themselves just to appear more desperate to victims. Some of these extreme deceivers have been known to make use of their own family members in this form of deception; they turn their children to drug addicts so as to use them in their fraud. There is no measuring the depth of money-related deceptions.

Another common branch of deception is the area of marital status. Some people hide their marriage background because they have the intention of seducing a new target. This can either be for financial gain or sexual pleasure, or other reasons are best known to the manipulator. There are some men who have multiple wives spread out across the world but these wives do not know about each other. This kind of deception, however, has become harder since the popularity of the internet which gives people the opportunity to check up on other people on social media. The best deceivers, regardless of the internet, have been able to expertly hide their tracks and keep each fake wife away from the other successfully.

Alternatively, there are some people who choose to appear falsely married where in actual fact they are not. This kind of deception can occur for various reasons. A couple who is considered married is usually trusted that that which is yet to tie the knot. Some people lie about being married because they are seeking for ways to either evade tax or gain insurance payment. Another common deception in this regard is the creation of a deceased husband or wife to gain people's sympathy and, often, their money as a result.

Many people are deceptive about their criminal background. This is due to the fact that it is almost impossible to be trusted professionally or personally if you are found out to be an ex-convict. An instance is a situation where a woman meets a man who has committed a grievous crime in the past. It is often rare for the man to reveal his past to the woman mainly due to the fear that the woman may end their relationship on discovering the truth. Strangely, such kind of reticent to reveal ones past criminal activity is not related to dark psychology; but if he hides the truth with a further intention of harming the woman in future, then such deception is considered dark.

Manipulators often feel that deception is a perfect way of hiding the abnormality in them. This prevents their victims from knowing the kind of person they truly are until the damage has already been done. For instance, when a person who uses dark psychology is only interested in another person mainly for sex, they know this focus is likely to be a red flag to their victim, and so they will take up the deception. They may either lie or make the victim see that their true intention is love and commitment. The victim eventually falls for this deception; and as soon as the manipulator gets what he wants, he discards the hurt victim like a piece of rag and moves on to other interesting catch.

Deception makes it easy to deploy solutions for detecting and responding to threats —important in this age of staff shortages. Deception not only strengthens defenses with early and accurate engagement-based detection but also plays a critical role in deterring attacks with visibility tools to assess likely attack paths, time-lapsed maps of attacker movement, and integrations for accelerated incident response.

While cyber attacks grow in number and sophistication, deception-based technology is providing accurate, scalable detection and response to in-network threats. Organizations increasingly are turning to deception to close the detection deficit and to gain an advantage over attackers with the ability to perform counterintelligence, increase their costs, and slow their attacks.

Lying is often the most chosen form of deception. It is always employed when manipulators discover that their victims are fallible to falsehood and are unable to discover the truth. This may be because the victim is a generally trusting person or that the manipulator has systematically and carefully worked on their victims over time until they lower their guard. Great manipulators usually have a backdoor to every plan they try to initiate; they often have a "Plan B" whenever they exercise their dark deception.

Deception through lies is usually planned to the last details. A skilled deceiver tries to merge their lies with the truth in such a way that it is hard to sift the lies out. A manipulator may tell a story that is 90% true and 10% false. The victim will see the story as totally true and will not have any means of separating the falsehood from the truth because they are blended together so perfectly.

Implying is a more covert form of falsehood than all-out lying. Implying involves opening that something false is true rather than boldly insisting it. If someone wants to deceive a victim about the amount of money they have then they could either lie or imply. A lie would be something like "I am highly successful. I have made a lot of money," whereas the manipulator knows that this is far from being the case. Implying, however, may take the form of "It's so difficult having to handle things with my accountant. Trying to reduce my tax bill takes a lot of my precious time". In this manner, the manipulator has acted in a way that implies they are wealthy without flatly stating it, even though they have no two nickels to rub together.

There are a variety of deception solutions available that range from very simple traps to fully automated deception platforms. While individual deceptions offer benefits within their approach, this post focuses on the features common to the distributed deception platforms available on the market that are most actively sought out based on their comprehensive detection and response to advanced threats.

Fundamentally, deception is designed to detect attackers when they conduct reconnaissance by moving laterally from the initially compromised system, and when they seek to harvest credentials from other systems. The assumption with deception is that no one should be engaging with the deception servers, decoys, lures, or bait because they provide no production capabilities that employees would access. Deception assets aren't advertised to employees, so any reconnaissance activity is a red flag and any engagement should prompt immediate action to prevent attackers from escalating their invasion.

Deception technology plays an instrumental role in changing the asymmetry of attacks. However, for deception to work, you need authenticity and attractiveness to fool savvy human attackers. Active Directory credential verification authenticates deception credentials as attractive targets. The deception that runs real operating systems and provides customization to match the production environment will appear authentic and trick attackers into revealing their presence. Facades built on emulation can be identified quickly and avoided by attackers. Dynamic behavioral deception techniques improve deception with machine learning that adapts to the behavior of the network, applications, and device profiles and continually refreshes to remain attractive.

Additionally, adaptive deception lets organizations reset the deception synthetic network on demand. If you're suspicious of attack activity, resetting the attack surface will avoid attacker fingerprinting that could be used to mark and avoid decoys, create uncertainty, and increase the likelihood of an attacker making a mistake. The increased complexity and cost of restarting will slow an attack and serve as a deterrent, driving the attacker to start over or seek out an easier target.

Deception-based detection is designed to detect in-network attackers early, regardless of the attack vector. Unlike other forms of detection, the solution does not require time to learn the network and is effective upon deployment. The network, endpoint, data, application, and Active Directory deceptions work collectively to detect lateral movement, credential theft, man-in-the-middle efforts, and Active Directory attacks.

Today's threat landscape and attack surfaces are ever-changing, and detection methods must adapt to provide early detection of threats at the endpoint, and as they move through the network. Comprehensive deception technology scales to the evolving attack surfaces and detects threats throughout user networks, remote office/branch offices, and data centers, and supports data migration to the cloud as well as specialized networks such point-of-sale systems. Out-of-band deployments provide the best operational efficiency and scalability, and agentless endpoint deception simplifies deployment and manageability. If your organization uses an endpoint detection and response solution, look for vendors with integrations that provide automated deployment and integrated management options.

Deception platforms with attack threat analysis will save time in automating the analysis and correlation of indicators of compromised information, which can then be used to accelerate incident response. Threat intelligence and forensic evidence reporting let organizations capture and catalog all attack activity to support understanding of the attacker's objectives, which can lead to better overall security. Deception solutions capture attacker behavior and through integrations share the full tactics, techniques, and procedures of the engagement with firewalls, security and event management systems, network access control products, and endpoint devices. These integrations also empower automated blocking and isolation of infected endpoints.

Through the use of files that contain fake sensitive data and beaconing technology that calls back when accessed by attackers, counterintelligence can be gathered on which types of files were stolen and for insight into where the data ends up.

Deception slows the attack as threat actors get lost in the deception environment while thinking they are escalating their attack. The use of adaptive deception creates complexity for the attacker by dynamically changing the perceived attack surface on attackers, increasing their cost, and acting as a deterrent. Notably, this ability to obfuscate the attack surface has proven itself with pen testers, who have also fallen prey to the deception environment and been tracked for days, only to find themselves defeated.

In addition, high-interaction deception for ransomware can slow down an attack by 25x or more. Deception-mapped drives lure attackers and feed them reams of fake data to keep them busy while the infected system is isolated from the network.

Manipulators often choose the implications because they give them the chance of plausible deniability. If the victim accuses the manipulator of lying, the manipulator can respond that they did not lie, and they are technically correct.

The omission is a deliberate failure to mention something that is true or important. The omission is different from other forms of deception like lies and implications since the latter use falsehood to hide the truth. The omission is simply ignoring the truth and leading the victim away from it, or even giving such victim the chance to ask questions related to the topic of omission. One sure way omission is practiced is by creating an "emotional fence" around a situation. This is a moment when skilled manipulators mention that some particular periods of their lives, or situations, are too painful for them to dwell upon. Talking about them would open up old wounds they have been trying to heal. The victim, out of compassion for the deceiver, will avoid talking about it.

Fraud is regarded as the most criminal form of deception used by those who make use of dark psychology. Imagine fraud to be something like a lie on steroid. Rather than lying about things from their past, a dark deceiver will present false documents, stories, and other evidence to support their lies.

However, they do this in a more subtle way though. They don't just scream about what they have achieved as the false documents have revealed but instead they leave the documents in strategic places where their victim is sure to discover them. They know that if they appear too insistent about their claims the victim might suspect that there's something wrong, that they are not entirely being truthful. Suspicious victims like that may embark on their own personal investigation of the manipulator without the knowledge of the receiver.

Now, even fraud is one of the most common forms of deception since the popularity of the computer and internet connection. Manipulators are now able to use professional-grade software to quickly and easily make realistic-looking documents of almost any type. Frauds of that nature can be carried out for either professional or personal reasons. A common instance is a situation where people have been able to obtain jobs by presenting false identity, stolen from a company, and then disappeared before their identity can ever be discovered. Personal fraud also includes some scary stories such as people with HIV spreading the disease with the help of falsely produced certificates of clean sexual health.

Deception in relationships often leads to a feeling of distrust and betrayal between partners. People often expect partners, relatives, friends to be truthful all the time, and when this trust is broken due to deception, it is usually very hard to regain the lost feeling.

6

BRAINWASHING

If other dark psychology techniques are mere bullets released from a gun towards a particular person, brainwashing is a nuclear weapon capable of turning a whole city to ruins. Brainwashing is the slow process of replacing a person's idea about identity and belief with new ideas that are intended to suit the purpose of the person doing the brainwashing. A brainwasher can use the same technique of controlling a single person on a wider group of people at the same time. Brainwashing is the process that turns atheists into suicide bombers. It has been tried, tested and proven over the years to be effective in almost any scenario.

The starting point of any form of brainwashing is the state of mind of the victim. This is the bases upon which the rest of the process is laid. Brainwashing is not something that can be carried out anyone. It requires the intelligent identification of someone who is seeking something or trying to find a meaning to their own life. Therefore, people who have had their reality shaken up by recent happenings around them are the major target for brainwashers. Many Western men who have traveled to become terrorists in Syria, and succeeded in detonating suicide bombs, have done so after the loss of loved ones. When their world loses its meaning, the brainwasher uses the opportunity to step in and provide answers to those things the victims seem to question in a violent or murderous ideology.

As soon as a brainwashing victim is identified, either in person or through the Internet, the real process of brainwashing thus begins. The brainwashers will come across as calm and friendly people who have the interest of the victim at heart. Imagine being homeless and being befriended by a celebrity. This is how the process of meeting their brainwasher for the first time feels for a victim. The brainwasher will start by creating a feeling of camaraderie between themselves and their victim. They start slowly but surely reeling the targets in, gradually into their webs. The victims will not know what hit them. The brainwasher will create a superficial similarity in such a way that the victim will feel that they have something in common with the manipulator. For instance, they will create an illusion of shared past experiences that have similarities with those of their victim. The brainwasher can go as far as providing their victim with gifts and some money to make them feel relaxed around their manipulator. It also gives their victim a sense of gratitude and indebtedness to their brainwashed.

A brainwasher may gather a lot of secretive information about their target; these pieces of information can be dirty, shameful or criminal. The brainwasher holds the information on their victim, either secretly or confrontationally; anything that would make the victim submit totally to them. However, most of these pieces of information are rarely used by skilled manipulators in a threatening way; no, they don't resort to blackmail. They use the information cleverly. For instance, if a victim, after divulging secret details to the manipulator, begins to walk away. The brainwasher may try to bring them back by saying something like "If you think I cannot help you anymore, then I think I will release the information I have to the authorities so that they can give you better help." If it is said with all sincerity, the victim will not see it as blackmail; instead, they will believe you are really concerned about them and eventually submit back.

During the Korean War, Korean and Chinese captors reportedly brainwashed American POWs held in prison camps. Several prisoners ultimately confessed to waging germ warfare -- which they hadn't -- and pledged allegiance to communism by the end of their captivity. At least 21 soldiers refused to come back to the United States when they were set free. It sounds impressive, but skeptics point out that it was 21 out of more than 20,000 prisoners in communist countries. Does brainwashing really work in any reliable way?

In psychology, the study of brainwashing, often referred to as thought reform, falls into the sphere of "social influence." Social influence happens every minute of every day. It's the collection of ways in which people can change other people's attitudes, beliefs, and behaviors. For instance, the compliance method aims to produce a change in a person's behavior and is not concerned with his attitudes or beliefs. It's the "Just do it" approach. Persuasion, on the other hand, aims for a change in attitude, or "Do it because it'll make you feel good/happy/healthy/successful." The education method (which is called the "propaganda method" when you don't believe in what's being taught) goes for the social-influence gold, trying to affect a change in the person's beliefs, along the lines of "Do it because you know it's the right thing to do." Brainwashing is a severe form of social influence that combiness all of these approaches to cause changes in someone's way of thinking without that person's consent and often against his will.

Because brainwashing is such an invasive form of influence, it requires the complete isolation and dependency of the subject, which is why you mostly hear of brainwashing occurring in prison camps or totalist cults. The **agent** (the brainwasher) must have complete control over the **target** (the brainwashee) so that sleep patterns, eating, using the bathroom and the fulfillment of other basic human needs depend on the will of the agent. In the brainwashing process, the agent systematically breaks down the target's identity to the point that it doesn't work anymore. The agent then replaces it with another set of behaviors, attitudes, and beliefs that work in the target's current environment.

While most psychologists believe that brainwashing is possible under the right conditions, some see it as improbable or at least as a less severe form of influence than the media portrays it to be. Some definitions of brainwashing require the presence of the threat of physical harm, and under these definitions, most extremist cults do not practice true brainwashing since they typically do not physically abuse recruits. Other definitions rely on "nonphysical coercion and control" as an equally effective means of asserting influence. Regardless of which definition you use, many experts believe that even under ideal brainwashing conditions, the effects of the process are most often short-term -- the brainwashing victim's old identity is not in fact eradicated by the process, but instead is in hiding, and once the "new identity" stops being reinforced the person's old attitudes and beliefs will start to return.

There are psychologists who say the apparent conversion of American POWs during the Korean War was the result of plain-old torture, not "brainwashing." And in fact, most POWs in the Korean War were not converted to communism at all, which leads to the question of reliability: Is brainwashing a system that produces similar results across cultures and personality types, or does it hinge primarily on the target's susceptibility to influence? In the next section, we'll examine one expert's description of the brainwashing process and find out what makes an easy target.

In the late 1950s, psychologist Robert Jay Lifton studied former prisoners of the Korean War and Chinese war camps. He determined that they'd undergone a multistep process that began with attacks on the prisoner's sense of self and ended with what appeared to be a change in beliefs. Lifton ultimately defined a set of steps involved in the brainwashing cases he studied:

1. Assault on identity
2. Guilt
3. Self-betrayal
4. Breaking point
5. Leniency
6. Compulsion to confess
7. Channeling of guilt
8. Releasing of guilt
9. Progress and harmony
10. Final confession and rebirth

Each of these stages takes place in an environment of isolation, meaning all "normal" social reference points are unavailable, and mind-clouding techniques like sleep deprivation and malnutrition are typically part of the process. There is often the presence or constant threat of physical harm, which adds to the target's difficulty in thinking critically and independently.

We can roughly divide the process Lifton identified into the following stages:

- Assault on identity: You are not who you think you are. This is a systematic attack on a target's sense of self (also called his identity or ego) and his core belief system. The agent denies everything that makes the target who he is: "You are not a soldier." "You are not a man." "You are not defending freedom." The target is under constant attack for days, weeks or months, to the point that he becomes exhausted, confused and disoriented. In this state, his beliefs seem less solid.

- Guilt: You are bad. While the identity crisis is setting in, the agent is simultaneously creating an overwhelming sense of guilt in the target. He repeatedly and mercilessly attacks the subject for any "sin" the target has committed, large or small. He may criticize the target for everything from the "evilness" of his beliefs to the way he eats too slowly. The target begins to feel a general sense of shame, that everything he does is wrong.

- Self-betrayal: Agree with me that you are bad. Once the subject is disoriented and drowning in guilt, the agent forces him (either with the threat of physical harm or of the continuance of the mental attack) to denounce his family, friends, and peers who share the same "wrong" belief system that he holds. This betrayal of his own beliefs and of people he feels a sense of loyalty to increases the shame and loss of identity the target is already experiencing.

- Breaking point: *Who am I, where am I and what am I supposed to do?* With his identity in crisis, experiencing deep shame and having betrayed what he has always believed in, the target may undergo what in the lay community is referred to as a "nervous breakdown." In psychology, "nervous breakdown" is really just a collection of severe symptoms that can indicate any number of psychological disturbances. It may involve uncontrollable sobbing, deep depression, and general disorientation. The target may have lost his grip on reality and have the feeling of being completely lost and alone. When the target reaches his breaking point, his sense of self is pretty much up for grabs -- he has no clear understanding of who he is or what is happening to him. At this point, the agent sets up the temptation to convert to another belief system that will save the target from his misery.

One of the most brutal side effects of brainwashing is a victim's loss of identity. One of the features of many cults is that those who are newly initiated into their groups are often given new names, usual names of their own choosing, not the new initiate's. By giving them new names, their former identities begin to slowly fade away from them. What they used to believe in will start to evaporate from their minds. When it is deftly carried out by the skilled brainwasher, the victim will start to doubt that the old identity existed in the first place, or they start to imagine that the old identity was nothing but a shattered glass in the depth of their mind whose pieces are yet to be picked up. The major objective of brainwashing is not only to alter a victim's opinion, but it's also to change their behaviors. Law-abiding citizens who have no heart for trouble can be brainwashed into becoming psychopaths, rapists, murderers, and armed robbers. There are different cases of brainwashed young people. They have been manipulated by religious extremists to strap explosives on themselves, walk to crowded people – people who they have never met before, people who have never done anything to hurt them – and detonate bombs, killing themselves and a multitude of other innocent people. The devastating effects of 9/11 still linger in our hearts till today. A lot of people who were not supposed to die were killed that day because some terrorists had been brainwashed into carrying out the carnage.

Post-traumatic stress disorder is often the eventual outcome of brainwashing; a person who has just been rescued from the clutches of a brainwasher will suffer massive PTSD and will require a lot of help in de-brainwashing before all the ideals they used to believe in a return to them. However, it will still take a long time for them to live a normal life again. If they are not given proper care and attention, victims of brainwashing can return to that dark side out of their own volition; because that is the only world that makes sense to them. It is very hard for a brainwashed victim to see their leader as an evil person most victims usually worship their brainwashers as if they are gods, and whatever anyone else tells them differently will be seen as absurd.

7

APPLICATION OF HYPNOSIS

The first thing you need to know is that hypnotism truly exists. It's not a myth, it's not a fictional concept or a magical display. There are real hypnotists and they are armed with powerful techniques to use on chosen targets. Hypnotism is the ability to make suggestions to someone that goes from the conscious to the subconscious. The ability for one to make a deep suggestion to someone while they are in a state of vulnerability grants hypnotic dark manipulator a high level of power over their victims.

Hypnotism can take the form of both verbal and non-verbal suggestive practices. Often, the forms of suggestion are very subtle and therefore very difficult to detect. Hypnotism works on the deepest level of a human mind. A person who is able to break into another's consciousness through hypnotism will be able to easily their victim without raising any form of suspicion on themselves.

The Tactics of Hypnotism

There are various types of hypnotic tactics, and there are many variations of these types. These variations offer an insight into the things to be conscious of. Instances of how each tactic can be applied shall be provided wherever possible to give an awareness of how hypnotists operate around us and still go undetected all the time.

Forms of hypnosis go back through history nearly as far as history itself. Even the earliest reported forms of deep meditation from India and Persia are considered to have been analogous to what we now refer to as self-hypnosis. Even the ancient Greeks are believed to have had practices comparable to Hindu sleep temples, where people would go to essentially become hypnotized to be put into a relaxed state as a presumed medical cure. But the history of hypnotism is associated with one name more than with any other: the 18th-century German physician Franz Mesmer.

You probably already know that we get the term "mesmerize" from the name of Mesmer, but what you may not know is that the practice of mesmerism has virtually nothing to do with anything that Mesmer himself actually did. As a physician working with the current state of medical science in the 1700s, Franz Mesmer didn't have much to go on. Like other researchers of his day, Mesmer put forth ideas that were not very sound scientifically. His particular theory was a form of vitalism — the idea that living beings are distinguished from inanimate objects by some kind of "life force" — that he called animal magnetism. Like most other forms of vitalism proposed over the centuries, Mesmer's animal magnetism postulated that living beings were connected by a sort of energy flow, which Mesmer called magnetic fluid. One of his treatments, which he popularized while practicing in Paris, was to use his hands to govern the flow of magnetic fluid through a patient, in lengthy and relaxing sessions, intended to cure some ailment.

It was those who followed Mesmer's work who coined the term mesmerism, but the practice was splintered into a number of unrelated directions. Magnet therapists called their procedures mesmerism. Spiritual healers in Russia called their procedures mesmerism. New Age healers in America called their practice mesmerism. Clairvoyants in England called what they did mesmerism. The connection to what we now call hypnotism came in 1841 when a traveling mesmerist who gave stage shows was going around London putting people into trances, calling it by Mesmer's term animal magnetism. Dr. James Braid, a surgeon, happened to catch one of these shows and had the opportunity to examine one of the subjects who had been rendered unable to open his eyes. He concluded, rightly it turned out, that the person was indeed in some different state of consciousness. Braid was fascinated and researched the phenomenon voraciously. In 1843 he published his findings in a book that he titled *Neurypnology*. It was Braid who coined the term hypnosis.

Braid's book, which may fairly be called the seminal work of modern hypnotherapy, was surprisingly in line with today's understanding of hypnosis. Braid had quickly taught himself to hypnotize patients by having them fix their gaze upon an object held in front of their foreheads, in such a position that it put a strain upon the eye muscles and required great concentration to maintain. He would speak to them calmly during the procedure, and once he observed their pupils dilate, he ascertained that they were hypnotized. This part of the process has since become known as the induction phase. As a doctor, he repeatedly found hypnotism useful as a treatment for what he called nervous complaints. He was able to successfully hypnotize patients and induce restful sleep, reduce muscle spasms and pain, and treat other symptomatic conditions.

Braid's basic technique has been revised many times, and one of today's most popular versions was developed in the 1950s at Stanford University, as the Stanford Hypnotic Susceptibility Scales. It's a series of twelve short tests to gauge just how hypnotized you really are, scored on a scale of 0 (not at all) to 12 (completely). They are responses to simple suggestions like immobilization, simple hallucinations, and amnesia. Most people score somewhere in the middle, and nearly everyone passes at least one of the tests. There's even a script you can follow to hypnotize anyone and put them through the scales, with a little bit of practice.

Not only do people score very differently, but there's also been little progress made in predicting what types of people are most susceptible. Subjects' suppositions about their own susceptibility don't correlate at all with test scores. Supposed predictors like intelligence, creativity, desire to become hypnotized, and imaginativeness also have no correlation. Most likely, you yourself are a decent candidate who will score near the middle of the scale, regardless of whether you think you will or not.

At least one study has found a physiological difference in subjects who score highest on the Stanford scales. In 1999, grad student James Horton at Virginia Tech took eight people who scored a median of 11 and ten people who scored a median of 2 and took a look at their brains with an MRI. The high scoring group had a frontal section of the corpus callosum called the rostrum that was 32% larger on average than that of the lower scoring group. While interesting and suggestive of the value of further research, this was a small sample size and there may have been other factors.

In 2001, six staffers from *Scientific American* magazine who had never been hypnotized before underwent the test at their office in New York. It turned out they fit the demographic as well as anyone: their scores ranged from 3 to 8, and they reported the inability to move parts of their bodies, auditory hallucinations, and one even was made to forget everything that happened during his session — despite his best efforts — until being told that he could suddenly remember it all again.

So this raises the question of what hypnosis can actually do. It has real applications in medicine and in psychotherapy. In medicine, it has surprisingly been proven to be quite effective at pain management, in many clinical trials. One survey of 27 such trials found that 75 percent of some 933 patients found some pain relief from hypnosis. It has been shown that pre-surgical hypnosis can reduce the amount of anesthesia needed, and thus it also reduces the time needed in recovery and the severity of related side effects like nausea. It can reducestress-related hypertension. In fact, virtually all of the symptoms related to stress can be successfully mitigated in susceptible patients.

Many of us wonder about the common usages we hear about in psychotherapy, like stopping smoking, weight loss, or recovering lost memories. These are generally overblown. We like to think that we can go to a hypnotherapist who will make us no longer desire cigarettes or food, and snap like magic, the problem is solved. This is completely fictitious, as are most magically easy solutions in life. Whether hypnotherapy is effective at all in long-term behavior modification is something of an open question. Weight loss has shown good promise, but studies of using hypnosis to stop addictive behavior such as smoking or drug abuse have been much less successful. The difference is probably that weight loss is a matter of willpower alone, whereas addictions such as nicotine have additional physiological factors. Regardless, virtually all authorities agree that hypnosis should only be used to supplement conventional psychotherapy, and should not be the only tool relied upon.

The idea of recovering lost memories is highly controversial and is no longer accepted as reliable. Hypnotherapists would lead the patient through age regression, to have them relive and re-experience a traumatic event. It is true that the focused, relaxed state does enable very strong and realistic recollections, but what we've learned is that these recalled experiences, though vivid, are no more accurate than any other memories. Similarly, a dream can be extremely realistic, but as we know, dreams don't necessarily reflect reality in the slightest. It's essentially the same imaginative mechanism in your brain that creates dramatic and lucid dreams that creates the perception of a relived moment in age regression hypnosis. The prevailing view is that the subject is not actually reliving what happened, but rather is realistically imagining what it was probably like way back when based in part on whatever recollections remain. Today, in many jurisdictions, hypnotically recovered memories are no longer admissible in court as evidence, since they've been proven to be too unreliable.

The biggest irony is that stage hypnosis, as practiced by showmen in front of audiences, is sometimes more real than these popular notions about clinical hypnosis. (We're discounting the stage hypnotists who use plants in the audience, or who whisper secret instructions to the subjects, or who employ another chicanery not related to hypnotism.)

Stage hypnosis generally is real hypnosis, just an extremely glib example of its most basic function. Think back to the show that James Braid witnessed, where a subject found himself unable to open his eyes. In all probability, that performance was the same exact thing that showmen do today. The basic program is to take a group of people and hypnotize them through a basic induction phase, much like Braid described. The hypnotist selects a few people from this group, and administers something akin to an abbreviated Stanford scale, selects those who respond best, and dismisses the rest. A weakness with stage hypnotism is that there are always some subjects who are only pretending to go along and perform according to audience expectations. However, as with the *Scientific American* staffers, plenty of stage hypnotism subjects report actually losing simple abilities during the show (forgetting their name, being unable to move, or experiencing hallucinations such as seeing people naked), *but only so long as they were consciously willing to go along.*

A lot of these shows end with the hypnotist laying a subject between two chairs and standing on her like a bridge, making it appear that hypnotism has given her super strength. The facts are that no such superpower becomes available during hypnosis, and he's simply positioning the body and the chairs in a way that would make it possible anyway. But it's unfair, and factually inaccurate, to dismiss all stage hypnotism as fake.

The experience of hypnosis can vary dramatically from one person to another. Some hypnotized individuals report feeling a sense of detachment or extreme relaxation during the hypnotic state while others even feel that their actions seem to occur outside of their conscious volition. Other individuals may remain fully aware and able to carry out conversations while under hypnosis.

Experiments by researcher Ernest Hilgard demonstrated how hypnosis can be used to dramatically alter perceptions. After instructing a hypnotized individual not to feel pain in his or her arm, the participant's arm was then placed in ice water. While non-hypnotized individuals had to remove their arm from the water after a few seconds due to the pain, the hypnotized individuals were able to leave their arms in the icy water for several minutes without experiencing pain.

The human brain can be likened to an iceberg. The part of the iceberg that is visible above the surface of the water represents the known and understood aspects of cognitive function such as thought. The larger deeper parts of the ice hidden below the water represent parts of the brain that are not easily accessible. Dark hypnotists target their efforts towards the hidden portion of the iceberg, the one that is fairly inaccessible to external forces.

There are two types of suggestion employed by hypnotists; they include the silent and verbal suggestions. Both types of hypnotic method appear in a variety of different forms. The type of hypnotism a manipulator chooses to use depends solely on a variety of factors. Some manipulators will carry out the form of hypnotism will create the most impact on their victim's particular psyche. Verbal suggestion is often very difficult to detect. Sometimes, dark hypnotists are able to implant suggestions into their victim's mind by using words that sound familiar to other innocent words.

If a hypnotist is trying to create a suicidal feeling in the mind of their targeted victim, they may replace the true command of "You want to die" as something similar sounding such as "You want to dine". The hypnotist would speak the words "You want to die" clearly but in a manner that would hide the true content. For example, the hypnotist could talk about an upcoming trip and state "You have to check out the local restaurants, you want to die, somewhere that is popular but picturesque". The victim's mind would absorb the suggestion of death without consciously understanding why.

A hypnotist tone of voice and the choice of words is another technique of verbal suggestion. Some hypnotists will carefully learn the pace and style of delivery a particular victim uses when they are expressing something serious and disturbing.

Suggestion can also take the form of the nonverbal approach. This can be through the hypnotic manipulator's body language or even cues they place in their environment. Political leaders have made use of such tactics in ways such as changing their hairstyle to convey a different intention during speeches. The human mind is easily vulnerable to even the smallest hints and cues.

The environmental stimulus is another form of the nonverbal suggestion among the hypnotist's toolkit. The environmental stimulus situation is like a child being summoned to the principal's office. The location alone is enough to send you into a feeling of panic because you have learned to associate the location with panic and problem. Hypnotists are able to use this same concept to devastating effect in adult life.

Hypnotism does not bring the same effect on every person it is tried on. Some tend to be more influenced by hypnotists than others. Although the exact level of a vulnerability is complex and hard to simplify in a single sentence, it boils down to the idea of vulnerability.

Vulnerable people are more likely to be agreeable to the suggestion that people who are less vulnerable.

The people most vulnerable to hypnotism are those who have had some past experience that was life-changing, and such events have reduced their certainty. A person who has just come out of a romantic relationship lost someone, or lost a job will be vulnerable to suggestion. This is due to the fact that the human brain seeks understanding.

A hypnotist looking to use their powers to gain financially, they might seek out a victim such as a rich, recently bereaved widow. They will then associate their own self with the feeling of security and comfort while increasing the widow's general feelings of loss and weakness. Eventually, the hypnotist is the victim's only escape from her own personal hell.

Neuro-linguistic programming (NLP) is a technique that is powerful even in the hand of the most well-meaning person. Those within the world of business and philanthropy are some of the most common advocates of the technique and principles offered by NLP. Placing such techniques in the hands of people ready to use the dark psychology to take advantage of others is like placing a nuclear weapon in the hands of a psychopath; imagine the destruction such a person can excite. Understanding the major techniques used by practitioners of dark psychology offers insight into the way they can be deployed to devastating impact.

Anchoring is an NLP technique that involves linking an emotional state to some form of external stimulus. Hypnotists are able to induce a powerful emotion in a victim and then link it to a stimulus such as physical gesture or tone of voice. The most dangerous hypnotists will apply the principle of anchoring on their victim for a prolonged period of time to create a variety of different anchors in the psyche of their victim without the victim having the slightest inkling of what is going on.

Reframing is the art of controlling the way ambiguous information is perceived. Hypnotists can apply the reframing method to manipulate the way their victims think. Consider a situation where a hypnotic manipulator has influenced a victim to no longer spend time around, or communicating with, a particular person. The victim may state feelings of sadness or loss related to this interpersonal change.

Future pacing is the closest thing to the psychologically manipulative time travel. Future pacing allows a skilled manipulator to lead their victim on a mental journey into the future and influence behaviors and responses that will occur in the actual, chronological future that exists independent of the victim's reality.

8

SEDUCTION USING DARK PSYCHOLOGY

Seduction and sexual conquest are one of the most common methods of dark psychology. Almost everyone has had a friend who has been seduced through the use of the dark psychology, and there may be some time you have applied the dark psychology to your own gain in the past.

The sex drive of the human being is one of the most powerful urges in the anatomy, and the inability to fulfill it when it is needed can lead to sadness and desperation. This is why some people find it difficult to control themselves around people of the opposite sex; it is one of the major reasons why some people resort to rape because they know of no other method to satisfy their urges at the time but to forcefully do it. A lot of famous historical figures have been known for their frequent and full fulfillment of their sexual urges. Political, traditional, even religious leaders, have been given the most exquisite of women as a reward for their elevated statuses.

King Henry 8 is an example of one of the most powerful seducers the world has ever had. His appetite for women was so strong that he created a movement that allowed him to marry as many women as he wanted. He also dominated the lives of all his wives that they dare not go against his wishes. He had had those who had disobeyed him beheaded and had gone further to marry more to replace them. His success among the women of his time was due to his own knowledge of the application of dark magic on people under him.

The use of dark magic in the pursuit of seduction is neither bad nor good, depending on the method of application deployed, or the impact it has on the person being seduced. Seducers using dark psychology have an advantage because they understand how the human mind works, and they use this understanding as a weapon. A lot of people who have applied the principle of dark psychology into the dating world have found it to be mindblowing and they realize that following the conventional rule of dating has been a mere waste of their precious time all the while. People apply the dark psychological seduction into the dating process with one of three objectives in mind – to help the people they seduce, to hurt the people they seduce, or to basically help themselves. The first reason might seem far-fetched at first. You may be wondering why people would go into seduction with the aim of helping the people they are seducing. It seems illogical, but it's possible since it is assumed that all seducers are selfish and only after their own desires.

You will be surprised to discover that the major principle of true seduction is "leave them better than the way you found them". With this viewpoint in mind, a true seducer will not work towards breaking the heart of the person they are seducing. Both the seducer and the seduced can benefit from the relationship in the long run, and if it ends, no one would feel like the other has cheated them. To enjoy a seductive lifestyle and make sure you leave the person better than you have found them, the first step is never to lie to the person you are seducing, and you should not mislead the person either. Most people with selfish aims will lead their victims by promising the world and offering nothing in the long run. True seducers do not make promises they cannot keep. Instead, the simply make the person enjoy the moment while it lasts.

The attitude of someone who goes about using the psychological seduction with selfish intent and not caring about the feelings of the person being seduced can have a devastating boomerang effect on the seducer. People who go about seducing other people with a carefree attitude always invite problems to themselves. These kinds of people often end up in entrapping situations where unwanted pregnancies may arise and they will spend the rest of their lives paying child support. In some worse situations, some may invoke the wrath of scorned lovers which, ultimately, may cause the lover to kill them out of spite or jealousy. Therefore, the game of psychological seduction must be carefully played or it may result in mortal consequences.

A planned seduction technique gives the seducer the confidence of certainty of knowing what to do next when any situation arises, because such a situation may have been foreseen from the beginning of the seduction. However, it can also pose a problem for the seducer because the person being seduced might not follow the path they are being led. Most unskilled seducers often think that human beings are like computer programs that must always follow a charted course. They fail to know that every human being has a mind of their own and they are free to follow their own intuition regardless of how strong the seduction may be. Therefore, the natural seduction approach is the one that is most effective. Do not struggle to make things work your own way because it may lead to disaster instead, let things take their own patterns and then go with the flow. Do not enter the world of the dark psychological seduction with magical expectations, it does not work that way. Freely express your emotion and gently move with the tides.

The typical view of seduction throughout history is that the man is often the aggressor and the woman plays a passive role. However, inverting this can lead to a powerful outcome. Some men have discovered that allowing themselves to become the prize, the one being chased, has helped their seduction intentions. Female psychological seducers can use the inversion to great effect when they assume the role of the aggressor and making dominating steps towards people of the opposite party. And it has been discovered that some men find aggressive ladies highly sexually-appealing, and they enjoy being the passive ones and submitting to their seducers' ideals. These female seducers usually have the feelings of empowerment that they have never had in their lives all through their dating process because they were too accustomed to being the dominated lot.

A lot of people enter the world of psychological seduction with the intention of breaking themselves free from the shackles of monogamy that have always held them down against seeking adventures. This approach is sometimes known as polyamory – a form of an open relationship between the two parties; it can be between a husband and his wife, or a seducer and the seduced. This system usually leaves no feeling of sadness or regret between the two parties because it is something they have agreed on. The dark psychological seducers, in this manner, will be able to pursue their sexual or romantic desires in such a way that is effective, liberating, honest and open. A seducer would not have to feel like they are hurting another person by their actions.

Another important technique in the world of seduction is the indirect approach. One common mistake people make in the world of seduction is by making unappealing icebreakers when trying to introduce themselves to the person they intend to seduce. Comments like "You are beautiful", "I like your eyes", "You like the movie, right?" are clichéd icebreakers and should thus be avoided by serious seducers because the women you are telling them to are likely to have heard them a thousand times in the past, and they automatically switch off their interest in you as soon as those words escape from your mouth. Whenever a seducer makes use of such lines it suggests that they are bland and boring, a great turn off to the potential target.

Using openers that are indirect are a lot more preferable to the clichéd ones. An indirect opener is that form of an icebreaker that brings about an interaction without conveying any form of sexual undertone. This is often used in the form of an intriguing question. For instance, a seducer making use of the indirect opener may ask "My friends and I are having an argument about who lies more between the men and the women. What is your stand?" This brings about a conversation and suggests to the seduced that a seducer is an interesting person who is interested in nothing more than a nice conversation. Indirect openers have the advantage of eliminating any possibility of rejection. Someone using an indirect opener is not offering themselves to the person they wish to seduce and so they are hardly rejected. Social proof is another technique in dark psychological seduction. Popular people are usually found more attractive than unpopular ones. It is human instinct to assume that if a person is popular then there is something likable about that person. Nobody would want to be seduced by some creepy loner whom nobody likes and has no friends.

In the application of social proof in psychological seduction, showing is usually more effective than telling. Many people are fond of talking about their success in such a way that it comes off as bragging or some form of unappealing behavior. It is better to simply be at a table in a bar or club with a group of interesting people and having interesting conversations. For instance, a psychological seducer in a club sees a girl he wants to talk to. Rather than directly approaching the person he wants to seduce, he simply approaches someone else first, starts a conversation with the wrong person and then later move to the original target and starts to interact with the intended person. This not only removes the perception of loneliness that might otherwise have existed but also strikes a feeling of jealousy between the two women.

Appearing as something of a challenge is a form of dark psychological seduction that many daters have still not learned to master. A lot of people make the mistake of being too eager and available. An example is a man who calmly waits while some girls in a bar or club ignore him completely or a woman who puts up with some form of disrespect from the person they are with. The opposite of the display of this form of the low standard is showing how challenging a person can be.

Walking away from a seduction target if needed is a way of adopting the "challenging" principle. If the target is being cheeky or sassy, the seducer can playfully say "you're done" and turn to walk away. Most times, the target would be amazed by this conventional behavior and enjoy interacting with a person who has standards and self-confidence.

Some psychological seducers are able to harness dark psychological traits such as elements of psychopathy in pursuit of their romantic aims. One of the features of a psychopath is the ability to not feel fear when interacting with other people. Most men and women are paralyzed by the fear of rejection from someone they are romantically interested in. To overcome the fear of rejection is by being rejected time and time again and eventually realizing that rejection is very bad after all. Psychological seducers know that it is better to be the person who tried and failed than being the one who didn't have the confidence to try at all. Naturally, the less a person fear rejection, the less that rejection actually occurs. Being confident and calm when interacting with someone new is a way of keeping the fear of rejection in check. The more a person gets rejected, the less the person fear rejection in the future. This becomes an actual success and less rejection eventually. This principle works for everyone. You only fear what you have not tried; when you try it, you find out it is not scary after all.

9

MIND GAMES USING DARK PSYCHOLOGY

The mind game is a concept many people may claim to recognize in their everyday lives, but only a few people are able to accurately understand what mind game truly is. It is just as many people say "I feel depressed" without meeting the right psychological definition for the term depression.

There are some people who associate a wide range of normal behaviors to mind games. If someone is teasing them and hinting at some kind of surprise, they will assume the person is playing mind games on them. This is a half-truth, at least in the world of dark psychology. The intentions of a person playing genuinely mind games are not very noble, friendly or positive, as the case may be. Therefore, such safe games such as teasing and surprises fall outside the realm of mind games.

If innocent games do not mind games in the sense of dark psychology, then what really are? Mind games are any type of psychological plot from the manipulator towards the victim they are intending to play the game on. This game usually threatens the sanity and stability of the chosen target. This kind of manipulation is different from the other types because this time around the manipulator is most often toying with the victim. The manipulator is less interested in the outcome as they are in the other kinds of manipulation, and they often have less regard for the gravity of the situation on the selected target.

A dark mind game can, therefore, be assumed to be the one played by the manipulator on the victim with the sole aim of deriving amusement and pleasure without respecting the victim's state of mind or wellbeing. Depending on the kind of mind game, the intention is often to test the victim and explore their psyche, just as a child would try out a new toy. The best dark psychology mind games are played out without their true nature becoming obvious; this, of course, can make the form of manipulation very hard to detect.

While exploring the difference between dark mind games and those that are innocent, motivations behind them are analyzed. The kinds of motivation that comes with the dark manipulative mind games can, therefore, be fully explored.

The major reason for exercising mind game on another person is to manipulate the victim into performing a behavior or thinking or feeling a certain way. The manipulator, in this situation, may feel that their other forms of manipulation may not be very effective and therefore attempt to try other less obvious forms of the manipulation, which, of course, include the art of playing mind games on a chosen victim. The manipulator may decide to influence their victim in this manner for their own sick amusement and fun. This occurs when the manipulator tries to seek pleasure as well as influence due to their deployment of the mind game.

The specific types of influence that can be achieved by playing the mind games will be further detailed. Basically, mind games are effective for the reduction of a victim's certainty and psychological strength in a very subtle manner that is hard to determine

Influencing a victim is not the major reason behind the playing of the mind games. A lot of manipulators play the mind games only as a form of entertainment, and no deeper reason is involved whatsoever. Manipulators explore and derive pleasure from planning a way of impacting a target's psychology and watching as the victim surrender to their intentions. Such manipulation is similar to a form of sociopathic detachment. Manipulators of this level often ignore the fact that their victims are also humans with feelings and thought; instead, they see their victims as mere play-objects they can choose to use as they wish. Their victims, to them, are just like a system that exists to be figured out or even manipulated just for the heck of it. This form of manipulation is particularly dangerous and borders on the precipices of insanity by the manipulator and the victim that falls under this kind of manipulation hardly get out of it. Most victims can be driven to suicide just to amuse the person playing the game with them. Their minds are totally shattered and they are filled with the loss of self-identity.

In some cases, dark psychological mind games are played as a form of learned behavior instead of representing any form of familiar intention on the side of the manipulator. This occurs when the manipulative person has already been exposed to such mind games all through their entire lives and therefore knows no other method. This process may be seen as harmless but it is not. For the fact that someone automatically does evil does not mean that they are absolved of the morality of doing better. Usually, the manipulators who play dark mind games without having to consider their intentions are the most dangerous ones. They know nothing but the dark side, and must, therefore, whet their appetites for the dark.

It is highly necessary to observe the different specific kinds of mind games. A lot like the overall concept of the mind games, the kinds of specific games people often play have both the innocent and the dark variations. Understanding the instances of dark psychology and the ones applicable to our day-to-day lives is important in understanding this branch of dark psychology.

Ultimatum is a situation where one person presents another with a severe choice. "Do this…or this will happen" is an example of an ultimatum. Other examples include "Quit smoking…or I will leave you" or "Lose weight…or I will see other people." From these instances, we can conclude that ultimatums are any kind of request that is similar to a demand. The use of the ultimatum is one of the major tools in the mid games of dark psychology; however, not every ultimatum should be considered a mind game.

The factors that can determine whether an ultimatum can be considered "dark psychology" are the kinds of people issuing the ultimatum, their motive for doing so, and the gravity of the ultimatum itself. Each of these factors will be explored to provide a detailed picture of the manipulation tactic of the ultimatum and how to apply it.

The individual issuing the ultimatum is an important factor in determining whether an ultimatum is evidence of dark psychology or not. In the situation of a legitimate, harmless ultimatum, the person issuing it may always have a genuine, honest care about the person they are trying to help.

Such honest and the caring individual could be a spouse, sibling or generally a relative. However, the fact that someone falls into any of these three categories does not mean their ultimatum is automatically devoid of the dark psychology. As a matter of fact, dark psychology is usually more effective when it is carried out by family members rather than strangers, or outsiders.

The motive behind the execution of the ultimatum is another important factor on how to understand it. People who implement the ultimatum with good intention are actually trying to make the life of the person they are issuing it on a lot better; they are trying to help, in their own way, the persons they care deeply about. This, if followed according to command, will improve the lives of the victims and ultimately make better persons out of them. Some well-meaning ultimatums may include such expressions like "Don't drink too much or I won't be around you anymore" or "Let's hit the gym or we won't have any more kids". These kinds of ultimatums are directed with the sole aim of helping someone make better decisions that will have a positive impact on their lives.

It is difficult to determine the intention of an ultimatum, however, and this is why it is not very easy to differentiate a darkly manipulative ultimatum from the intention behind it. The nature of the ultimatum is usually the best way to figure out whether it is manipulative or not. Dark manipulation, however, usually requires that the person act out against their own self-interest or making decisions that abuse their personal morality. In aiming for this result, the manipulator has the intention of discovering the extent to which their victim is willing to go against what they truly believe in. In contrast, fair ultimatums will not cause a person to perform the things that will cause them or other people harm, or anything that threatens their conscience.

People issuing dark psychology ultimatum often have no valid status within their victim's life. For instance, the ultimatum imposed may be on someone having an illicit romantic affair with, either the victim's boss or someone who has too much psychological influence and control over the life of a victim. They can also take valid roles in the victim's life.

A victim who has an aversion to taking alcoholic drinks for either health or ethical reason may be manipulated by another through the issuance of an ultimatum. The manipulator may note this aversion and decide to make the victim break it simply for their own twisted amusement. The manipulator will, therefore, use the idea of alcohol as a foundation of the ultimatum with which to manipulate the victim's conviction. Some of these ultimatums are "Drink with me or I will not let you touch me" or "Either take a shot or don't appear at the party. We don't welcome teetotalers."

Some extreme ultimatum can involve the intention of making the victim inflict on themselves [or others] harm, murder or suicide. The manipulator may say something like "stab yourself in the arm or I will slit my own throat." A manipulative girlfriend may place an ultimatum on her boyfriend by telling him to "Kill that man or I'm going to walk away and you will never see me again." In the most extreme manner, some people are manipulated into taking their own lives under the illusion of a suicide pact. Once the victim is dead, the successful manipulator, of course, refuses to carry out their side of the agreement.

People in happy, peaceful or stable romantic relationships usually do not need the feeling of the constant threat that their relationship might crash in the future. Skilled dark manipulators usually have the knowledge of this principle and they, therefore, do everything to plant such negativity for their own twisted pleasure. By sowing the seeds of chaos, instability, and negativity in a thriving relationship, the manipulator always ensures that the relationship is threatened as strongly as possible; and the do this by making their victims as powerless as possible.

One of the most effective methods of manipulation mind games used within a romantic concept to result in anxiety is The Eternal Breakup. It is the persistent and prolonged use of the threat of walking out of a relationship. This may take the idea of implied breakups, promised breakups or actual breakups that are not really carried out. Careful consideration shall be placed on each of these tactical manipulations.

Implied breakups are those forms that do not actually involve the verbal threat of a breakup, the manipulator does not mention it but all their actions and reactions give the impression of the breakup. Rather than mentioning it, the manipulator hints at the breakup through some symbolical means to instill the idea in the mind of their victim. The manipulator may causally make mention of some future plans that exclude the person they are with. This may give the indication that a breakup is possible, or imminent as the case may be. A manipulator planning to hint the possibility of a breakup can make such a statement as "Well, this won't continue for long". Any statement that makes the victim doubt the durability of the relationship without actually mentioning the idea of a breakup is known as an implied breakup.

The promised breakup, on the other hand, is standing in the middle of an actual breakup and an implied breakup. This time around, the manipulator makes an open threat to their victim and declares that they have the intention of breaking up with their victim in the nearest future. A manipulator may issue such statement as "I am going to leave you soon and I won't have to put up with this nonsense anymore." A situation where the manipulator addresses the idea of a breakup without actually carrying out the threat is known as the promised breakup.

The actual breakup is the final instance, and it is usually the most devastating of all the three eternal breakup mind game. This is where the manipulator carries out the threat but not really follow through with it in the end. A manipulator may decide to pack their things but decide to stay when they witness their victim's sadness. They may break up with their victim but not really follow through on it after a series of pleading and begging from the devastated victim.

The overall intention of the mind game is meant to terminate the feeling of certainty and assurance in the mind of a victim, and to reduce their power on the manipulator; instead, the power is placed in the hand of the manipulator. This kind of mind game can be akin to an evil test of the litmus paper on the outcome of the relationship. By breaking up with their victim over and over, the manipulator will be able to ascertain the extent to which the victim is willing to put up with being manipulated. The manipulator is also able to portray themselves as the considerate one for agreeing to not break up with the victim if the victim is begging for the relationship not to be terminated.

The outcome of someone that has been exposed for long to the subject of an eternal breakup can be devastating.

They are often likely to develop trust issues in the long run and lack the ability to trust anyone else in any other situation. The eternal breakup manipulation on a victim can destroy the victim's family and professional lives, which is exactly what the manipulator wants. After a long period of being broken up with, the victim is likely to become almost a subservient slave to their manipulator, doing anything they are told to avoid another breakup, which they now utterly dread. Oftentimes, the manipulator loses interest in the relationship after completely shattering the will of the victim. They move on to seek new adventures and leave a destroyed life in their wake.

The hard-to-get mind game can easily be confused for the normal healthy behavior. Some differences show that the hard-to-get mind game can be evidence of dark psychology. The first step in the understanding of the hard-to-get concept is to know when it is innocent or evil.

The innocent psychological use of the hard-to-get can involve the following: A person will want to create the idea of being a challenge to someone they fancy romantically. They will pretend not to be always available. They will turn down dates, refuse to reply texts or calls quickly. This intention is usually for keeping the second party interested and they will have an eventual happy relationship.

The hard-to-get that borders on the dark psychology deployment is a lot more brutal and dangerous. The particular period when this mind game is employed is different from its innocent application and the motive is usually many million miles apart. Manipulators that make use of the dark psychology will exercise the hard-to-get during the relationship and not at the inception of it. The intention, however, is not to result in a positive outcome since their intentions are far from the victim's wellbeing.

The major reason the hard-to-get concept can be innocently deployed is that it does not directly violate any expectation at the beginning of the relationship, as the party playing hard-to-get can easily decide not to go on with the relationship at the early stage, and such decision will not deeply hurt anyone, so to speak. But when someone becomes elusive and evasive in the course of the relationship, then fear and doubt begin to set into the mind of the partner; the effect of the hard-to-get becomes scary and unbearable.

A person may play hard-to-get out of a relationship by being unreliable after both partners have made an agreement on starting a relationship. This is an inversion of the conventional method. Ordinary but normal relationships are often elusive at the beginning but become firmer as the relationships grow. A manipulator may be firmer at the beginning of the relationship to bring about a sense of connection to the union, and then they become less and less emotionally available in the course of the relationship, just when they are very certain that their victim is already "hooked" to their apron string.

A person who plays hard-to-get in a relationship makes the partner try to chase and reconnect with the person trying to pull away. This automatically places the power in the hand of the manipulator.

10

MIND CONTROL ON VICTIMS

The mind is a person's safe haven, and when it is invaded, the person becomes utterly vulnerable to the invader. Some people believe that the mind cannot be claimed by an external person. They believe strongly that the concept of mind control is nothing but a myth.

Indeed, a lot of people like to think they are absolutely the controller of their own thoughts when it is obvious that they are not. A good example is given in subliminal advertising. The first case of mind control in subliminal advertising may have occurred in 1957. While a movie was being shown in a theatre, a special message appeared on the screen. 'You are thirsty', it read. It appeared and disappeared so fast that no one realized that it was there. But before the movie ended, it had been flashed for about a thousand times. At the end of the film, almost all the theatergoers went to the lobby and purchased soft drinks. In that first experiment, which had been carefully regulated by researchers in the mystery of the mind, the subliminal message on the theatergoers had been delivered with a machine known as the tachistoscope. The machine was later patented by a company in New Orleans called the Precon Process and Equipment

Corporation in October 1962. The machine, the tachistoscope had a high-speed shutter and could flash a message as fast as twelve times a minute at **1/300** of a second. The image that flashed on the screen was too short for the conscious mind to perceive, but the subconscious was taking a full record of the happening. Within the first six-week of the test, over forty thousand movie-goers were exposed to two messages: "Drink Coca-Cola" and "Hungry? Eat Popcorn". The outcome of these experiments showed the efficacy of subliminal advertising on the human mind the sales of popcorn rose sixty percent, and the sales of Coca-Cola skyrocketed almost twenty percent. The subliminal advertising had influenced people into buying the advertised products on the screen even though they were neither hungry nor thirsty. Yet, the audience in the cinemas would claim that they were in full control of their own minds. The experiment carried out had shown that the man could be easily controlled or manipulated.

Our minds are easily vulnerable to influence and control. When you are watching a horror movie, your mind and emotions are being influenced by the camera angle, the background music, and the lighting. Although you know that what you are seeing isn't real, your brain still responds to the prompts it is given. Sometimes you find yourself cowering in fear because of the gory scenes and the brutality being displayed on the screen. If the brain can be influenced so absolutely by the thing we have chosen and are also aware of, how do you think the influence would be of an experienced dark psychological manipulator?

A mind control undetected is the most dangerous kind of control in existence. If someone is aware that their mind is being controlled, then that person can reject such in various ways, it could be through verbal, mental or physical rejection.

They will thus avoid the controlling individual as much as possible so as not to fall victim to them again. Most people would run at a person they know is capable of invading their minds and taking control therein. If the mind controller is not detected or known, then the victim will not be able to fight off this psychological manipulation.

Taking control of another person's mind can be done in two methods – the interpersonal interaction, and the use of the media. Usually, media mind control is possible for large companies (just like the case of the Coca-Cola and Popcorn illustration given in the previous pages). Nowadays, however, the introduction of laptops and smartphones has placed the power of media control in the hands of the most brutal manipulators walking the face of the earth.

Undetected mind controllers usually appear to be cowardly and logical than other kinds of manipulators, but in contrast to the impulsive psychopaths, detected mind controllers have the likelihood of acting only after careful deliberation. To control someone's mind in an undetectable way is no small feat; it demands the application of deliberate knowledge and application. Mind controllers are usually patient people because they take their time to develop the growth of their control over an individual and their minds. They often fear the possibility of getting discovered so they conceal their intentions as much as they can. They are the puppet masters in the shadows who continually pull their victims' string with impunity.

There are specific methods used by skilled manipulators to control the minds of their victim in a way that is undetected. The interpersonal and media methods are the manipulator's toolkit. Examples of how such techniques can be applied to an individual shall be provided.

One of the most essential tactical techniques of undetected mind control is discovering a victim with a goal. It has been scientifically proven that a person who is in need is more prone to falling victim to undetected mind control than those who feel comfortable and are at peace with themselves and their society. This can range from an apparently irrelevant want like feeling thirsty or hungry, to a largely relevant goal like carving love and affection.

A person who is searching for someone in a crowd will sift out those who are not necessary to their goals and focus themselves on the one on whom their interest is aligned. The brain is like a similar case, too. If it wants anything, it will direct a person towards that thing, even if the individual is unaware that a form of control is taking place. The best controllers of the mind will cleverly find out what their target's goals are, then he further attempts to manipulate them with these in mind. When a person's brain has been designed to be desperate for something, it will immediately make a suggestion on the specific thing to choose.

If a mind controller is able to find someone with a yearning for something in their life, especially the desire for some deep emotional needs, the manipulator will be able to easily control the minds of these kinds of people. For instance, a person who has recently suffered a breakup in a romantic relationship will crave for companionship. The mind controller can easily step in and pretend to be the savior their victim wants, whereas they will turn out to be their destructions.

This is a verbal form of mind control that remains undetected; it is a very mild form of the dark psychology due to the fact that it gives the manipulator an assortment of built-in "get out clauses" should the target become wary of them. The most important key to this form of mind control is to take away the choice a target may have as regards to a particular circumstance while making the target feel that they are in control all the while.

This choice pattern is similar to the popular sale method referred to as the choice close. We shall consider an example that will illustrate this process of control, observing the difference between someone acting in a perfectly rational way and a dark manipulator whose interest alone is to serve their own intention even at the detriment of other people's happiness.

Imagine the case of a woman being asked on a date. Normally, a regular guy might come up with enough courage to ask his question, but lacking the confidence, he begins to stammer before the lovely woman. He then asks the question in a crude way: "Would you like to go out with me?" Such a question leaves a clear possibility of a negative response. This is the typical way things go for people who are ignorant of the application of dark psychology.

A person who knows how to control other people's minds in a manner which is undetected will take a different approach to the same scenario. They enjoy confidently charming their victim, to get them laughing and gradually breaking down the venerable walls they built around themselves. Then with full confidence, the clever manipulator pops up the question: "So am I taking you out on Thursday or Saturday?" A negative response, in this case, is highly unlikely.

The deceptive aspect of the technique explained above is that, unlike other forms of the mind control, like those supported by the media, there is no evidence of what a person has said for nothing is making a record of the speaker's statement. If the victim picks up on the restricting choice from the manipulator, the manipulator can respond in either of two ways – a denial or a reframe.

A denial gives the manipulator the opportunity to insist they do not offer a limited choice, and that the victim is remembering the wrong things, or even worrying too much.

A reframe gives the manipulator the chance to put the victim on the back foot by saying such stuff like "I can't believe you're analyzing my words so much. That really hurts me and makes me not want to open up to you." Both the denial and the reframe are both effective in their own ways – they both serve as emergency exits for the manipulator whose trick is discovered.

Our five senses can be as much as our enemies and traitors as much as they are our guides in life. The visual processing area of our brain is always very active, and it records things faster than all the other senses. The sense of sight is often prone to imagery and visual manipulation; which is a very powerful technique of the media mind control.

Originally, media was in the hands of companies and institutions. These manipulative entities were easily able to take over the visual, subliminal mind control. We are now living in the world of smartphones and videos; anyone can shoot videos and send them immediately. High tech manipulators are therefore able to allude people's fears to the images they see. For instance, if a manipulative boyfriend finds out that his girlfriend is afraid of spiders, he may "accidentally" place a book with the picture of a spider on its cover in the background during a video chat. The girlfriend is unlikely to consciously register the book's presence, but on a subtle, emotional level, she will be feeling its impact.

Sound is another sure way in which a person remains vulnerable to undetected mind control. Have you ever had a song stuck to your head? How easy was it to get rid of? The sound holds quite a powerful influence over you, even though you knew it was present. The power of audio manipulation is even greater when it is undetected. The experiment has shown that if restaurant customers are exposed to music from a particular region, they are more likely to order wine from that country. When questioned, they had no idea that something as simple as the sound had steered their decision.

Media mind controllers use sound in hiding words and phrases in songs and other media containing a soundtrack. Lawsuits have occurred which claim that musicians hide occult messages and references in their songs, and to ban them from doing so. This has happened with more serious impact beyond the world of entertainment media.

Some governments have used audio mind control as a form of brainwashing. In North Korea, people are forced to listen to patriotic songs at a regular interval.

The audio undetected mind control can be used by individual manipulators. There is a wide range of interpersonal influence methods with the use of auditory mind control of any type even if you know the tactics, it is still difficult to recognize them as being executed. This is due to their stealthy, underhand nature.

A creepy form of the auditory mind control is the art of subliminally influence a person during their sleep. There are tapes that are played in someone's sleep that enable them to quit the dirty act of smoking. A skilled mind controller is the evil equivalent of such advertised products. The manipulator takes advantage when a victim lets their guards down by sleeping. The manipulator will take this opportunity to implant their dark and devious commands in a person's ear and allow them to sink into the deepest layers of the brain.

Another kind of interpersonal auditory mind control is hiding words with similar sounding words or noises. In the movie American Psycho, genuine mind control was being displayed there. The major character in the movie, serial killer Patrick Bateman, blatantly tells his victims what he does: "I'm in executions and murders." When questioned about what he just said, he calmly responds, "I'm in acquisition and mergers." The subliminal influence, however, is already in the person's psychological recesses

A form of auditory mind control that both individuals and organizations can make use of include such sounds as the ones that are outside the range of human perception. Such sounds, which are particular frequencies, impart deep feelings of terror, unease, or dread into those who are exposed to them unknowingly. Although such sounds are widely applied in horror movies, some experienced mind controllers have successfully made use of sounds to impact the emotional stability of their victims.

11

CASE STUDIES ON DARK PSYCHOLOGICAL PRINCIPLES APPLIED

C ase studies offer information and insight on some of the most psychologically rare people that have ever lived. These case studies revealed in this chapter are not presented with the aim of glorifying the deeds the people involved have done or even judging them, instead, they are given with the sole aim of learning from them.

The Final Testimony of Ted Bundy

Ted Bundy is one of the most notorious serial killers the world has ever known. One interesting aspect of Ted Bundy is the number of articles published about him and his crimes on newspapers and magazines. The media helped make this man a celebrity with the way focus was given about him and his ultimate personality; his childhood, his education, his likes and dislikes – Ted Bundy became something like a household name. even Bundy's willingness to grant interviews and offer insight into his crimes and personality spur a lot of interest from the public. However, the level of hype and intrigues surrounding high-profile criminals often outweighs the gravity of their crimes. But Ted Bundy's case is not like that.

Indeed, no exact number of murders has been linked to Ted Bundy. He was charged with thirty cases of murders but it was hinted that he could have killed at least a hundred people. Even some analyst had discovered that Ted had lost count of the number of people he had killed.

During the time Ted Bundy was on death row after being sentenced to death, many articles and books were written concerning Ted's background, psychology and possibly what caused him to do what he did. Even after his death, a lot of post-humus analysis was taken about the famed mass murderer. Curious analysts wanted to understand how the mind of the notorious murderer worked and what motivated him to carry out all those gruesome murders. Indeed, a lot of sick psychopaths had been motivated by the actions of Ted Bundy; they studied articles written about the criminal and had tried to use his methods in performing their own evil deeds. Among the numerous interviews of Ted, he confessed that his early crimes had been unprofessional and sloppy. But he soon improved with time as he learned to be more careful, accurate and sure in his strikes. He learned to pick his victims out after careful studies. He grew up to become a methodological mass murderer.

Even while he was being interviewed, the way Ted Bundy's mind worked was hard to determine because he was fond of disguising the truth and could say anything if it was going to benefit him. He was known as a shapeshifter because he could disguise his appearance and lead people off his true identity. As skillful as Ted Bundy was able to conceal his true motivations, methods, and techniques for his world purposes, it showed how deeply dark his mind was, and his ability to use the dark psychological deception to attain his own aim

Deception is one of the most powerful traits Bundy had. He was skilled at interacting with people, especially his potential victims, trying to weigh them psychologically and physically before landing the mortal blows. He understood the power of public image and perception, and this is what he used as his tool. Anyone who encountered him found him to be a charming and attractive person, and they immediately lose their guards to him. The scary identification of the emotional coldness and utter lack of feeling that psychopaths like Bundy would have on their victim after giving them a sense of comfort and attraction before killing them in the most brutal way is remarkable. The feeling of detachment he often had after killing his victim showed how sadistic he was and how dark his mind had become.

Even while on death row, Bundy was still able to use his power of deception on the authorities. He was able to extend the dates of his execution with the hint of revealing the locations of the corpses of more of the people he had killed; he had seen it as a leverage to extend his own life and he had used it. To him, a corpse is nothing but a bargaining chip for the extension of his own life. Bundy is a testimony of how highly-intelligent a psychopath can be. He was able to evade arrest or detection for a long time because he understood the methods of law enforcement agents; he understood their psychology and the way they thought. Bundy also showed signs of sadism and narcissism by torturing his victims to death and then taking their pictures. In some cases, he made videos of his kills and referred to himself in the third person; that was how warped, and perhaps also lucid, his mind was.

And when he was eventually detected and hereby arrested, he did not show any feeling of remorse whatsoever.

The Narcissism of Saparmurat Niyazov

This man is famous for his ability to take advantage of the power vacancy created by the collapse of the Soviet ideology. He took over as the leader of Turkmenistan. His narcissistic display was manifested when he decided that he would be the president for Life of Turkmenistan. Afterward, he proceeded in renaming a particular month of the year after himself to reflect his own glory. He implemented laws that were in accordance with his own personal choice, such as deciding on how his citizens would appear and dress and changing the names of things to what he felt they should be called. One of the most remarkable of Niyazov's feats was the creation of a religious text that was meant to be given the same importance as the Holy Qur'an.

Insights Into Dark Psychology

People in power who have exhibited the traits of narcissism and dark psychology had been able to do what they did because they had been granted absolute power. Kim Jon Un, the current dictator of North Korea, had his own uncle executed for yawning in a meeting. The man was executed by the use of an anti-aircraft weapon capable of destroying fighter jets. A narcissist believes that they are a special kind of human beings like they are a rare breed, and so they feel they are superior to any other human being, especially someone of a different race.

Someone like Hitler is an example of such kinds of narcissistic people. His plan was to take over the entire world under his totalitarian Third Reich, and he nearly succeeded. His ultimate goal was the total extermination of the German Jewish population. Hitler knew how to manipulate the political system of the time as well as all the hearts and minds of all German people. His corpse was not discovered. Various speculations existed about his existence after the war. A strong suggestion arose that Hitler did not die in Germany. That he escaped Nazi Germany and fled to Argentina to live the rest of his life surrounded by fellow Nazi escapees.

Hitler believed strongly the maxim that it is better to be loved and feared, but if love is impossible, then feared rather than loved. Even after the carnage, Hitler excited during World War Two; he was regarded as the closest thing to the devil. Yet, Hitler was gifted in triggering the feelings of love, respect, and loyalty in the minds of people who listened to him. Each time he spoke in public, he was able to hold the people spellbound in such a manner that a lot of them were ready to die for him. An old woman who listened to one of his speeches had confessed that she had felt like she was seeing an angel speech when she watched Hitler.

Hitler was a strategic man who knew what he wanted, and what he didn't. He eliminated anyone who stood in his way on his quest to restore Germany back to its former glory. He had a very special and barbaric way of treating those unfortunate people in his concentration camps. These poor people were subjected to such terrible vice as medical experimentation, torture, and death by gassing or starvation.

Dark Psychology of Con Artists

Researchers are often surprised at how con artists have historically operated by applying the principles of influence which has been proven by modern science. A lot of infamous con artists have been discovered to be dark psychological influencers with a mastery of the principles that the modern world is only beginning to understand.

The application of the Ponzi scheme is still being used effectively till today, and millions, if not billions, of people, are still falling for it. The Ponzi name originated from a man named Charles Ponzi who was able to conduct a large-scale fraudulent investment on a lot of people. One remarkable feature of Charles Ponzi was the ability to maintain his cool and confidence when he found himself in a sticky situation. When a group of pissed-off investors arrived at the place of Charles Ponzi's office, rather than panicking, Charles was able to calmly placate the intending mob through his inspiring method of approach to them.

Another known con artist is a man named Gregor MacGregor. He was known for selling to rich people things that never existed. Common ridiculous stories of con artists selling the Eiffel Tower or the Brooklyn Bridge to wealthy people had been inspired by the actions of Gregor MacGregor in his prime. Gregor carried out his own operation by claiming that he was nobility from an archipelago that didn't exist. He would recruit people with wealth to fund an expedition to these imaginary islands. The reason MacGregor was so successful in his con was because he was so convincing to his victims; he knew how to play on their psyches and their egos to a detailed and thorough extent in such a way that even after trying to visit these islands and discovering that they never existed, the victims still defended Gregor in the press, simply because they did not want to appear to the public that they had been taken for fools by the man MacGregor.

A lot of lessons can be learned from the dark psychology of con artists. The ability to be able to exert a level of influence that even researchers have not been able to attain has set them apart from other forms of the dark psychological manipulations. They understand the psychology of the human mind and they take advantage of it effectively. Almost anyone can fall prey to the tricks of a con artist if the manipulator carries out his job expertly.

Ponzi, a form of con artistry, involves finding a victim with weakness and then ruthlessly exploiting such weakness. They carry out this deception in a way that betrays no doubt or hesitation whatsoever. Ponzi is a perfect way of carrying out a fraud with confidence. The best con artists are able to carry out their scams for many years without being discovered.

Faith healer, too, is also some form of con artists. Their application offers an insight into the suggestibility of their victims. These healers are so convincing that they tell their victims to eschew the normal medical treatment process and follow their own directives. Oftentimes, they persuade their victims to buy and use their own fake products and totally ignore the medical ones. Usually, these victims end up losing their lives. Even then, these healers are convinced, or they try to convince other people, that these victims died because they did not use the products as exactly as they have been instructed to do. Faith healers why so many people are susceptible to the influence of charismatic religious cults. Each time a strong spiritual belief is combined with a real-world need, such as the need to find relief from a particular ailment or pain, people can be driven to an extreme measure. And that is what most religious leaders take advantage of. In some parts of the world, there are more churches than those who attend them. Almost everyone is a religious leader who appears as someone capable of healing another because they have understood the gullibility of the mind of the average person. More surprisingly, these manipulated victims are ready to defend the ideals of their manipulators anywhere. Even after these rich investors had been deceived by MacGregor, after they had been financially exploited, their time wasted, made to look stupid, they still chose to defend MacGregor in public. This is evidence of the ingenuity of Gregor MacGregor. He understood that people who hold themselves in very high esteem in public, those who have high social status, rarely admit to being cheated or conned, because they are afraid that their pride may be bruised and they will look weak in the public eyes. Apart from publicly admitting the fact, they will also be unwilling to admit it in their own minds. Ironically, this is an example of how someone's narcissism can be used against them.

The Irony of Psychopathy

People have always associated psychopathy with negativity. The term 'psychopath' is an image of a person who is mentally unhinged and capable of committing any grievous crime. A person lacking motherly care right from childhood is likely to grow up into becoming a psychopath. However, such is not always the case.

Andy McNab is a person with such psychopathic trait but which many people would refer to as 'good psychopath'. MacNab was abandoned as a child, and he grew up into a life of petty crimes. He eventually joined the army and rose through the rank where he afterward joined Britain's elite SAS special forces unit. But after returning from the world of the armed forces, he turned out to be a successful author and playwright.

A person who is born with psychopathy and is lacking in opportunities and advantages, such a person is likely to become an unstable and dangerous person capable of carrying out horrible deeds, such as Ted Bundy. However, if a psychopath is able to direct their urge to the career they find suitable for them, the chance of them becoming successful is very high, such as Andy McNab.

So, basically, the Dark Psychology can be used for either of two purposes – the positive purpose or the negative purpose. And whenever you are applying these techniques you have learned, be conscious of the extent of impact you are willing to create on your target (i would not call them 'victim' at this juncture). You have to decide within yourself on which part of the fence you are choosing to sit. I wish you good luck in your adventures.

www.ingramcontent.com/pod-product-compliance
Lightning Source LLC
Chambersburg PA
CBHW060410290526
45791CB00002B/690